# 心理学
## 英和・和英
## 基本用語集

編著

小花和 Wright 尚子
安藤明人
佐方哲彦

福村出版

**JCOPY**〈出版者著作権管理機構 委託出版物〉
本書の無断複写は著作権法上での例外を除き禁じられています。複写される場合は，そのつど事前に，出版者著作権管理機構（電話 03-5244-5088，FAX 03-5244-5089，e-mail: info@jcopy.or.jp）の許諾を得てください。

# まえがき

　日常生活のさまざまな場面で、外来語が使われるようになっています。心理学の専門用語にも、カタカナで表記されるものが増えてきました。それは、外国語、とくに英語で書かれた論文の中から、心理学の基本用語として定着する概念や知識が次々に現れていることを意味しています。

　このように今日では、優れた心理学の論文の多くが、英語で書かれ発表されています。専門用語の意味を理解するために、その用語が提案されたオリジナルの英語論文を読むことは、必ずしも必要ではないかもしれません。しかし、用語を提案した研究者の考えや発想を理解し、用語が提案されるまでの背景を知るためには、オリジナルの論文を読むことが望ましいと考えられます。とくに心理学を専攻する大学生が、授業のレポートや卒業論文を書く場合には、それらの英語論文を読むことが必要となるでしょう。

　そこで、武庫川女子大学文学部心理・社会福祉学科では、英語で書かれた心理学の文献を講読する授業を実施しています。この授業は、英語自体を学ぶ授業ではありません。高等学校までに学習した英語の力も使いますが、それ以上に、大学で学び始めた心理学の知識を駆使しながら、英語で書かれた心理学の文献にまず慣れること、次に読み方を知ること、そして読む力をつけることを目的としています。

　ところが、この授業で多くの学生が最初にぶつかる壁は、心理学の専門用語の日本語訳でした。心理学の専門用語の多くは、一般的な英和辞書には載っていません。その用語が意味する概念を日本語で理解している場合でも、日本語に訳することができないために、文章全体の意味をうまくとらえられないのです。心理学専門用語の辞書には、英語の用語を載せたものもありますが、毎回の授業に持ち歩くことができるようなハンディなものは見あたりませんでした。

本書は，このような背景から，武庫川女子大学文学部心理・社会福祉学科の心理学担当教員が企画し，専門分野ごとに用語の選定を行い編纂したものです。大学生が英語で知っていることが望ましいと思われる心理学の基本的な専門用語1,644と人名223を取り上げました。心理学の分野や領域によっては，同じ英単語が異なる日本語に訳される場合もあるため，その日本語を用いることが多い分野や領域も示しました。ただ，こうした分野や領域は，おおよその指標に過ぎません。1つの日本語訳だけにこだわらずに，いくつかの日本語訳をあてはめながら考えることが，文章全体の意味をうまくとらえるためには有効でしょう。

　心理学を専攻し，授業のレポートや卒業論文の作成を控えている大学生の皆さんや，これから大学院に進学し本格的な研究を積み重ねていきたいと考えている皆さんに，日常的に活用していただければと思います。

　最後に，この用語集の出版にあたり，ご尽力くださいました福村出版株式会社の石井昭男社長と編集部の石井早苗氏に，心より感謝申し上げます。

2010年3月

武庫川女子大学文学部心理・社会福祉学科
編者　小花和 Wright 尚子
安藤　明人
佐方　哲彦

# 目　次

用語集の説明……………………………………… 6

人名集の説明……………………………………… 7

分野表……………………………………………… 8

## ◆用語集◆

英　語→日本語 …………………………………  9

日本語→英　語 ………………………………… 70

## ◇人名集◇

アルファベット→カタカナ …………………… 130

カタカナ→アルファベット …………………… 140

## 用語集の説明

### 英語→日本語
（1）心理学の専門用語の中で，大学生が英語で知っていることが望ましいと思われる用語をアルファベット順に配列した。
（2）英語用語の綴りは，アメリカ英語を主としている。イギリス英語綴りは（英），ドイツ語は（独）として示した。
（3）英語用語に付けられた（ ）は，その用語の略語を示す。
（4）略語，あるいは綴り違いは，＝ によって示した。
（5）英語用語とほぼ同じ内容を示す専門用語が他にもある場合には，→ で示した。
（6）英語用語と対をなす内容の専門用語については，⟷ で示した。
（7）同じ英語用語でも，適用される日本語が分野・領域によって異なる場合があるときには，8ページの分野表にしたがって，用いられることが多い分野・領域を示した。

### 日本語→英語
（1）「英語→日本語」の逆引きとして，日本語用語を五十音順に配列した。
（2）英語用語の綴りは，アメリカ英語を主としている。ドイツ語は（独）として示した。
（3）日本語用語に該当する英語用語が複数ある場合には，／で単語を区切った。
（4）日本語用語と同じ内容を示す専門用語がある場合に，⇒ で示した。
（5）日本語用語に該当する英語用語とほぼ同じ内容を示す専門用語が他にもある場合には，→で示した。
（6）英語用語と対をなす内容を示す専門用語については，⟷ で示した。

## 人名集の説明

### アルファベット→カタカナ
(1) 心理学,あるいは関連する学問における学者名の中で,大学生が英語で知っていることが望ましいと思われる人名を選択している。姓と名のアルファベット順に配列した。
(2) 姓のみをカタカナで表記した。なお,異なる読みがある場合には,( )で示した。
(3) 公開されている生誕年,没年を示した。非公開である場合には — によって示した。
(4) 心理学の中での主な活動分野を,8ページの分野表にしたがって示した。

### カタカナ→アルファベット
(1) 「アルファベット→カタカナ」の逆引きとして,カタカナ表記の人名を五十音順に配列した。
(2) 姓のみをカタカナで表記した。なお,異なる読みを,⇒によって示した。

## 分野表

| 分野記号 | 心理学分野・領域 |
|---|---|
| A | 歴史,原理・哲学 |
| B | 感覚・生理・神経心理,知覚・人間工学 |
| C | 学習・行動 |
| D | 記憶・認知,思考・問題解決 |
| E | 言語・コミュニケーション |
| F | 感情・動機づけ |
| G | パーソナリティ・知能 |
| H | 発達・教育 |
| I | 社会・産業・組織 |
| J | 臨床・障害,犯罪・非行・異常 |
| K | 方法・数理・統計 |

# 用語集
英語→日本語

## A

| | | |
|---|---|---|
| abandonment anxiety | 見捨てられ不安 | J |
| ability | 能力 | |
| absolute threshold | 絶対閾(いき) | B |
| abstract | （論文）要約，アブストラクト | K |
| abuse | 虐待 | J |
| abused-child syndrome | 被虐待児症候群 | J |
| acceptance | 受容 | J |
| accomplishment quotient (AQ) | 成就指数 | G |
| achievement motive | 達成動機 | F |
| Acquired Immunodeficiency Syndrome (AIDS) | 後天性免疫不全症候群，エイズ | J |
| ACTH | = adrenocorticotropic hormone | |
| acting out | アクティング・アウト，行動化，行為化 | J |
| action potential | 活動電位 | B |
| action research | アクション・リサーチ | K |
| active imagination | アクティブ・イマジネーション，能動的想像 | J |
| active listening | 傾聴，アクティブリスニング | J |
| acute psychosis | 急性精神病 | J |
| ad hoc | その場限りの，その場しのぎの | K |
| adaptation | 適応，順応，アダプテーション | BC |
| addiction | 嗜癖(しへき)，中毒 | J |

# ADHD

| | | |
|---|---|---|
| ADHD | = attention-deficit hyperactivity disorder | |
| adjustment | 適応 | C G J |
| adolescence | 青年期 | A H |
| adrenocorticotrophic hormone | = adrenocorticotropic hormone | |
| adrenocorticotropic hormone（ACTH） | 副腎皮質刺激ホルモン | B |
| affect | 感情→ affection | F |
| Affect-Infusion Model | 感情混入モデル | I |
| affection | 感情→ affect | F |
| affiliation motive | 親和動機 | F I |
| after effect | 残効 | B |
| after image | 残像 | B |
| age graded | 年齢級の | G H |
| agenda-setting | 議題設定 | I |
| agent | エージェント | G |
| aggression | 攻撃性 | |
| aging | エイジング，老化 | A H |
| agnosia | 失認（症） | B D J |
| agoraphobia | 広場恐怖 | J |
| AIDS | = Acquired Immunodeficiency Syndrome | |
| aim | （研究）目的→ purpose | K |
| Ajase complex | 阿闍世コンプレックス | J |
| alcoholic | アルコール依存症の | J |
| alcoholism | アルコール症，アルコール依存症 | J |
| alexia | 失読症 | B |
| alexithymia | アレキシサイミア，失感情表現症 | J |
| algorithm | アルゴリズム | |
| alternating play | やり取り遊び | H |

## ANOVA

| | | |
|---|---|---|
| alternative hypothesis | 対立仮説 | K |
| altruism | 利他主義，愛他主義 | C I |
| Alzheimer's disease | アルツハイマー病 | J |
| ambiguous figure | 多義図形，あいまい図形 | B |
| ambivalence | 両面価値，両面感情，アンビバレンス，両価性 | F H J |
| amentia | アメンチア，先天性精神遅滞 | J |
| American Psychiatric Association (APA) | 米国精神医学会 | |
| American Psychological Association (APA) | アメリカ心理学会 | |
| amnesia | 健忘（症） | D J |
| amphetamine | アンフェタミン<br>→ methamphetamine | B |
| amygdala | 扁桃体 | B D F |
| anal phase | 肛門期 | G H J |
| anal stage | = anal phase | |
| analogy | 相似 ⟷ homology<br>類推 | B<br>D |
| analysis of covariance | 共分散分析 | K |
| analysis of variance (ANOVA) | 分散分析 | K |
| anchoring effect | 係留効果 | D |
| androgyny | 両性具有 | J |
| anecdotal evidence | 逸話的証拠 | A K |
| anima | アニマ | J |
| animism | アニミズム | D H |
| animus | アニムス | J |
| anomie | = anomy | |
| anomy | アノミー | I J |
| anorexia nervosa | 神経性食欲不振症 | J |
| ANOVA | = analysis of variance | |

| | | |
|---|---|---|
| ANS | = autonomic nervous system | |
| anthropophobia | 対人恐怖 | J |
| anticipatory anxiety | 予期不安 | J |
| antisocial behavior | 反社会的行動 | H |
| antisocial personality | 反社会的人格 | J |
| anxiety | 不安 | |
| anxiety disorder | 不安障害 | J |
| anxiety neurosis | 不安神経症 | J |
| APA | = American Psychiatric Association | |
| APA | = American Psychological Association | |
| apathy | アパシー, 無関心, 無感動 | J |
| | 無気力→ helplessness | C J |
| aphasia | 失語（症） | B E J |
| apparent movement | 仮現運動 | B |
| approach-approach conflict | 接近―接近葛藤 | F |
| approach-avoidance conflict | 接近―回避葛藤 | F |
| apraxia | 失行（症） | B J |
| aptitude | 適性 | H I |
| aptitude test | 適性検査 | H |
| aptitude treatment interaction (ATI) | 適性処遇交互作用 | H |
| AQ | = accomplishment quotient | |
| archetype | 元型 | J |
| arousal | 覚醒, 喚起 | F |
| art therapy | 絵画療法, 芸術療法 | J |
| artificial intelligence | 人工知能 | B G |
| asocial behavior | 非社会的行動 | H |
| Asperger syndrome | アスペルガー症候群→ Asperger's disorder | J |
| Asperger's disorder | アスペルガー障害→ Asperger syndrome | J |

| | | |
|---|---|---|
| assertion training | アサーション・トレーニング，自己主張訓練 | J |
| assessment | 査定，アセスメント | |
| assimilation | 同化 | B |
| association | 連合<br>連想 | A B C<br>C D J |
| assumption | 仮説→ hypothesis | K |
| ATI | = aptitude treatment interaction | |
| attachment | 愛着，アタッチメント | H J |
| attachment relationship | 愛着関係 | H J |
| attention | 注意 | |
| attention-deficit hyperactivity disorder (ADHD) | 注意欠陥多動性障害 | J |
| attitude | 態度 | I |
| attribution | 帰属 | D I |
| audition | 聴覚→ auditory sense, sense of hearing | B |
| auditory sense | 聴覚→ audition, sense of hearing | B |
| author | (論文) 著者 | K |
| authoritarian personality | 権威主義的パーソナリティ | G I |
| autism | 自閉 (症) | J |
| autistic spectrum disorders | 自閉症スペクトラム障害 | J |
| autobiographical method | 自叙伝法 | J K |
| autogenic training | 自律訓練法 | J |
| auto-intoxication | 自家中毒 | J |
| autokinetic movement | 自動運動 | B |
| automatic process | 自動的過程 | D |
| autonomic dystonia | 自律神経失調症 | J |
| autonomic nervous system (ANS) | 自律神経系 | B |
| average | 代表値，平均→ mean | K |
| avoidance learning | 回避学習 | C |

| | | |
|---|---|---|
| avoidance-avoidance conflict | 回避―回避葛藤 | F |
| awareness | 気づき | J |
| axon | 軸索突起 | B |

## B

| | | |
|---|---|---|
| babbling | 喃語 | E H |
| Babinski reflex | バビンスキー反射 | B H |
| backward conditioning | 逆向条件づけ | C |
| basic encounter group | ベーシック・エンカウンターグループ | J |
| basic trust | 基本的信頼 | H |
| battery | バッテリー → test battery | K |
| Baumtest（独） | バウムテスト → tree drawing test | G J |
| Bayes' theorem | ベイズ理論 | K |
| behavior | 行動 | |
| behavior observation | 行動観察 | K |
| behavior therapy | 行動療法 | C J |
| behavioral counseling | 行動カウンセリング | J |
| behaviorism | 行動主義 | A |
| behaviorist approach | 行動主義アプローチ | A |
| behaviour（英） | = behavior | |
| belief | 信念 | |
| Bender Gestalt Test（BGT） | ベンダー・ゲシュタルト検査（テスト）→ Bender Visual Motor Gestalt Test | G H |
| Bender Visual Motor Gestalt Test | ベンダー・ゲシュタルト検査（テスト）→ Bender Gestalt Test | G H |
| beta wave | ベータ波 | B |
| between-subject factor | 被験者間要因 | K |
| BGT | = Bender Gestalt Test | |
| bias | かたより，バイアス，歪み | D |

| | | |
|---|---|---|
| bilateral transfer | 両側性転移 | C J |
| binge eating | 気晴らし食い，過食→ bulimia | J |
| binocular disparity | 両眼視差 | B |
| binocular vision | 両眼視 | B |
| binomial distribution | 二項分布 | K |
| biofeedback | バイオフィードバック | B C |
| biological response | 生理的反応 | B |
| birth trauma | 出産外傷 | J |
| blind analysis | 目かくし分析，ブラインド・アナリシス | J |
| body image | 身体像，身体イメージ | B J |
| body language | ボディ・ランゲージ，身体言語，身振り語 | C E |
| body schema | 身体図式 | B J |
| boomerang effect | ブーメラン効果 | I |
| borderless society | ボーダーレス・ソサイエティ | I |
| borderline case | 境界例 | J |
| borderline personality disorder | 境界性パーソナリティ障害 | J |
| bottom-up processing | ボトムアップ処理 | D |
| brain organic syndrome | 脳器質症候群 | J |
| brain storming | ブレインストーミング | J |
| brain waves | 脳波→ electroencephalogram | B |
| brainwashing | 洗脳 | I |
| breath-holding spells | 息どめ発作 | J |
| brief therapy | ブリーフセラピー | J |
| Broca's area | ブローカ領域 | B E |
| bulimia | 過食（症）→ binge eating | J |
| bullying | いじめ | H J |
| burnout | 燃え尽き，バーンアウト | I J |
| buzz session | バズ・セッション | D H I |

## bystander effect

| bystander effect | 傍観者効果 | I |

## C

| CA | = chronological age | |
| CAI | = computer assisted instruction | |
| canalization | 水路づけ | J |
| canonical correlation analysis | 正準相関分析 | K |
| career counseling | キャリア・カウンセリング | IJ |
| career development | キャリア発達，キャリア開発 | |
| carry-over effect | キャリーオーバー効果 | K |
| case conference | ケース・カンファレンス，事例検討会 | J |
| case study | ケース・スタディ，事例研究 | J |
| castration anxiety | 去勢不安 | J |
| CAT | = Children's Apperception Test | |
| categorization | カテゴリー化 | K |
| category | カテゴリー | |
| catharsis | カタルシス，浄化 | IJ |
| causal attribution | 原因帰属 | |
| ceiling effect | 天井効果 | K |
| central nervous system (CNS) | 中枢神経系 | B |
| central tendency | 中心化傾向 | IK |
| central vision | 中心視 | B |
| cerebellum | 小脳 | B |
| cerebral cortex | 大脳皮質 | B |
| cerebral palsy (CP) | 脳性麻痺 | J |
| cerebrum | 大脳 | B |
| character | 性格 | G |
| Children's Apperception Test (CAT) | 児童絵画統覚検査 | J |
| chi-square test | $\chi^2$検定，カイ二乗検定 | K |

| | | |
|---|---|---|
| chromosomal aberration | 染色体異常 | J |
| chromosome | 染色体 | |
| chronological age (CA) | 生活年齢 | G H K |
| chunk | チャンク | D |
| circadian rhythm | 日周期リズム | B |
| classical conditioning | 古典的条件づけ | C |
| classification | 分類 | K |
| client | クライエント，来談者 | J |
| client-centered therapy | 来談者中心療法 | J |
| client-centred therapy (英) | = client-centered therapy | |
| close relationship process | 親密化過程 | I |
| cluster | 群，クラスター | K |
| cluster analysis | クラスター分析 | K |
| CMC | = computer-mediated communication | |
| CNS | = central nervous system | |
| CNV | = contingent negative variation | |
| cocktail party effect | カクテルパーティ効果 | D |
| cocktail party phenomenon | カクテルパーティ現象 | D |
| code | コード化する，符号化する | K |
| coding | 符号化，記号化→ encoding | K |
| coefficient alpha | アルファ係数 | K |
| cognition | 認知 | |
| cognitive appraisal | 認知的評価 | F |
| cognitive behavioral therapy | 認知行動療法 | D J |
| cognitive consistency | 認知斉合性 | I |
| cognitive constraint | 認知的制約 | D |
| cognitive dissonance | 認知的不協和 | I |
| cognitive dysfunction | 認知機能障害 | J |
| cognitive function | 認知機能 | |
| cognitive map | 認知地図 | D |

## cognitive process

| | | |
|---|---|---|
| cognitive process | 認知プロセス | |
| cognitive psychology | 認知心理学 | |
| cohesiveness | 凝集性 | I |
| cohort | コホート | H I K |
| collage therapy | コラージュ療法 | J |
| collective behavior | 集合行動 | I |
| collective unconscious | 集合的無意識 | J |
| color | 色 | |
| color blindness | 色盲 | B |
| colored hearing | 色聴 | B |
| colour（英） | = color | |
| commitment | コミットメント，関与 | I J |
| communality | 共通性 | K |
| community | 地域社会，コミュニティ | I |
| community psychology | コミュニティ心理学 | |
| comparative psychology | 比較心理学 | |
| compensation | 補償 | |
| competence | コンピテンス | |
| competition | 競争，競合 | H I |
| complementary colors | 補色 | B |
| complex | コンプレックス | J |
| compliance | 承諾，応諾，コンプライアンス | I |
| compulsion | 強迫行為 | J |
| compulsive | 強迫的→ obsessive | J |
| computational approach | 計算論的アプローチ | D |
| computer assisted instruction（CAI） | コンピュータ援用学習システム | H |
| computer-mediated communication（CMC） | コンピュータを介したコミュニケーション | I |
| concept | 概念 | |
| concept formation | 概念形成 | D |

| | | |
|---|---|---|
| conceptually driven processing | 概念駆動型処理 | D |
| concomitant interview | 並行面接 | J |
| condition | （独立変数の要因における）条件 | K |
| conditioned reflex | 条件反射 | C |
| conditioning | 条件づけ | C |
| conduct disorder | 行為障害 | J |
| cone | 錐体(すいたい) | B |
| confederate | 実験共謀協力者，サクラ ⟷ naive participant | K |
| confidentiality | 守秘，秘密保持 | A |
| conflict | 葛藤(かっとう)，コンフリクト | F I J |
| conformity | 同調 | I |
| confrontation | 対決，直面化 | J |
| confusion | 錯乱 | J |
| congruence | 一致，適合 | J |
| conjoint counseling | 合同面接 | J |
| conjoint family therapy | 合同家族療法 | J |
| connectionism | コネクショニズム | B D |
| connotation | 内包 | D E I J |
| conscious | 意識の | |
| consciousness | 意識 | |
| conservation | 保存 | D |
| constancy | 恒常性 | B H |
| constant method | 恒常法→ method of constant stimuli | K |
| constellation | 布置 | J |
| constitution | 体質 | J |
| constraint | 制約 | |
| construct validity | 構成概念妥当性 | K |
| consultation | コンサルテーション | J |

## content validity

| | | |
|---|---|---|
| content validity | 内容的妥当性 | K |
| context | 文脈 | |
| contingency | 随伴性 | C |
| contingent negative variation (CNV) | 随伴陰性変動 | B |
| continuous reinforcement | 連続強化 | C |
| contrast | 対比 | B |
| control group | 統制群，対照群 | K |
| controlled process | 制御的過程 | D |
| convergence | 輻輳(ふくそう) | A H |
| | (眼球)輻輳運動 | B |
| convergent validity | 収束的妥当性 | K |
| conversion symptom | 転換症状 | J |
| coping | コーピング，対処 | B C D J |
| core identity | コア・アイデンティティ，核心的同一性 | H J |
| cornea | 角膜 | B |
| correlation | 相関 | K |
| correlation coefficient | 相関係数 | K |
| cortex | 皮質 | B |
| counseling | カウンセリング | |
| counselling（英） | = counseling | |
| counterbalancing | カウンターバランス | K |
| covariance | 共分散 | K |
| covariance structure analysis | 共分散構造分析 | K |
| CP | = cerebral palsy | |
| creativity | 創造性 | D |
| credibility | 信憑性(しんぴょうせい) | I J |
| criminological psychology | 犯罪心理学 | |
| crisis intervention | 危機介入 | J |
| criterion-related validity | 基準関連妥当性 | K |

| | | |
|---|---|---|
| critical period | 臨界期 | H |
| cross table | クロス集計表 | K |
| cross-cultural counseling | 異文化間カウンセリング | |
| cross-cultural study | 異文化研究 | K |
| cross-sectional study | 横断的研究 | H K |
| crowd | 群集 | I |
| crystallized intelligence | 結晶性知能 | G |
| cue | 手がかり | C |
| cult | カルト | J |
| culture shock | カルチャーショック | I |
| culture-general | 文化共通の | A G J |
| culture-specific | 文化特異の | A G J |
| cumulative frequency | 累積度数 | K |
| curiosity | 好奇心 | |
| custom | 慣習 | |
| cutaneous sense | 皮膚感覚 | B |
| cyclothymia | 循環気質 | J |

## D

| | | |
|---|---|---|
| DA | =dopamine | |
| DAM | =Draw-a-Man test | |
| DAP | =Draw-a-Person test | |
| dark adaptation | 暗順応 | B |
| data | データ | K |
| data driven processing | データ駆動型処理 | D |
| day dream | 白昼夢，白日夢 | J |
| debriefing | ディブリーフィング | K |
| deceive | 偽る | D H I J |
| deception | 欺き，偽り<br>ディセプション | D H I J<br>K |

| | | |
|---|---|---|
| decision making | 意思決定 | |
| declarative knowledge | 宣言的知識 | D |
| declarative memory | 宣言的記憶 | D |
| decoding | 復号化，符号解読 ←→ encoding | K |
| deduction | 演繹, 演繹法 ←→ induction | |
| defence mechanism（英） | = defense mechanism | |
| defense mechanism | 防衛機制 | F J |
| degree of freedom（*df*） | 自由度 | K |
| deindividuation | 没個性化 | I |
| delinquency | 非行 | |
| delirium | せん妄 | J |
| delusion | 妄想 | J |
| demagogy | デマ | I |
| dementia | 認知症 | G J |
| demographic trait | 人口統計学的特性 | I |
| denial | 否認 | J |
| dependence | 依存 → dependency | H J |
| dependency | 依存 → dependence | H J |
| dependent variable | 従属変数 | K |
| depersonalization | 脱個人化，離人症 | I J |
| depression | 抑うつ，うつ病 | J |
| depressive neurosis | 抑うつ神経症 | J |
| deprivation | 剥奪 | H |
| depth perception | 奥行き知覚 | B |
| depth psychology | 深層心理学 | |
| derealization | 現実感喪失 | J |
| description | 記述 | K |
| descriptive statistics | 記述統計学 | K |
| desensitization | 脱感作 | J |
| design | （研究，要因）計画 → experimental design | K |

| | | |
|---|---|---|
| destructiveness | 破壊性 | |
| development | 発達 | |
| | 開発 | G I J K |
| developmental acceleration | 発達加速現象 | H |
| developmental disorder | 発達障害 | H J |
| developmental dysgraphia | 発達性書字障害 | H J |
| developmental quotient (DQ) | 発達指数 | H K |
| developmental reading disorder | 発達性読字障害 | H J |
| developmental stage | 発達段階 | H |
| developmental task | 発達課題 | H |
| deviant behavior | 逸脱行動 | H I J |
| *df* | = degree of freedom | H I J |
| diagnose | 診断する | J |
| diagnosis | 診断 | J |
| Diagnostic and Statistical Manual of Mental Disorders (DSM) | 精神障害の診断・統計マニュアル | A J |
| diagnostic test | 診断（的）検査 | J |
| difference threshold | 弁別閾→ differential limen, discriminative threshold, just noticeable difference | B |
| differential limen (DL) | 弁別閾→ difference threshold, discriminative threshold, just noticeable difference | B |
| differentiation | 分化 | C H |
| directive counseling | 指示的カウンセリング | J |
| disability | （能力の）障害 | J |
| disabled child | 障害児 | H J |
| discourse | 談話 | E |
| discriminant analysis | 判別分析 | K |
| discriminant validity | 弁別的妥当性→ divergent validity | K |

## discrimination

| | | |
|---|---|---|
| discrimination | 弁別<br>差別 | I |
| discriminative stimulus | 弁別刺激 | B |
| discriminative threshold | 弁別閾(いき)→ difference threshold,<br>　　differential limen,<br>　　just noticeable difference | B |
| discussion | (論文) 考察 | K |
| displacement | 置き換え | J |
| disposition | 素質 | G |
| disruptive behavior disorder | 破壊性行動障害 | J |
| dissociation | 解離 | J |
| dissociative identity disorder | 解離性同一性障害 | J |
| dissonance | 不協和 | I |
| distal stimulus | 遠(えん)刺激 ←→ proximal stimulus | B |
| distracter | 妨害刺激 | D |
| distraction | 気晴らし | F J |
| distribution | 分布 | K |
| distributive justice | 分配的公正 | I |
| diurnal variation | 日内変動 | B J |
| divergent validity | 弁別的妥当性 → discriminant validity | K |
| divorce | 離婚 | |
| DL | = differential limen | |
| domestic violence (DV) | 家庭内暴力 | J |
| door-in-the-face technique | 譲歩的要請法 | I |
| dopamine (DA) | ドーパミン | B F |
| double bind | ダブルバインド, 二重拘束 | J |
| double blind test | 二重盲検法 (二重遮蔽法), 二重ブラインドテスト | K |
| double-barreled question | ダブルバーレル質問 | K |
| double-barrelled question (英) | = double-barreled question | |
| Down's syndrome | ダウン症候群 | J |

| | | |
|---|---|---|
| DQ | =developmental quotient | |
| Draw-a-Man test（DAM） | 人物画知能検査→<br>Goodenough Draw-a-Man test | G J |
| Draw-a-Person test（DAP） | 人物画テスト | G J |
| dream work | ドリーム・ワーク | J |
| drive | 動因<br>欲動 | B C F<br>J |
| drowsiness | 傾眠 | J |
| DSM | =Diagnostic and Statistical Manual of Mental Disorders | |
| dualism | 物心二元論 | A |
| dummy variable | ダミー変数 | K |
| DV | = domestic violence | |
| dysarthria | 構音障害 | J |
| dyslexia | 読字障害 | J |

## E

| | | |
|---|---|---|
| early childhood | 幼児期 | A H |
| early infantile autism | 早期幼児自閉症 | J |
| eating disorder | 摂食障害 | J |
| eclecticism | 折衷主義 | J |
| ectomorphy | 外胚葉型 | G |
| EDR | = electrodermal response | |
| educational counseling | 教育相談 | H J |
| EEG | = electroencephalogram | |
| effect | 効果 | K |
| effector | 効果器 | B |
| efficiency | 効率，能率 | C |
| ego | 自我 | G J |
| ego function | 自我機能 | J |
| egocentric speech | 自己中心語 | E H |

| | | |
|---|---|---|
| egocentrism | 自己中心性 | H |
| egogram | エゴグラム | G J |
| ego-identity | 自我同一性 | H J |
| ego-involvement | 自我関与 | I J |
| ego-strength | 自我の強さ ⟵⟶ ego-weakness | J |
| ego-weakness | 自我の弱さ ⟵⟶ ego-strength | J |
| eidetic image | 直観像 | B |
| eigenvalue | 固有値 | K |
| elaboration | 精緻化 | D |
| electrocardiogram | 心電図 | B |
| electrodermal response (EDR) | 皮膚電気反応 → galvanic skin response | B |
| electroencephalogram (EEG) | 脳波 → brain waves | B C |
| electroencephalograph | 脳波計 | B C |
| electromyography (EMG) | 筋電図 | B |
| embryo | 胎胚(たいはい) | |
| EMG | = electromyography | |
| emoticon | 顔文字 | I |
| emotion | 情動 | |
| emotion regulation | 情動制御 | F |
| emotional deprivation | 情緒剥奪(はくだつ) | J |
| emotional disturbance | 情緒障害 | J |
| emotional expression | 感情表出 | F |
| emotional intelligence | 情動知能 | G |
| empathy | 共感 | J |
| empiricism | 経験論, 経験主義 | A |
| encephalitis | 脳炎 | J |
| encoding | 符号化, 記号化 → coding ⟵⟶ decoding | K |

| | | |
|---|---|---|
| encounter | 出会い,エンカウンター | J |
| encounter group | エンカウンター・グループ,出会い集団 | J |
| endocrine gland | 内分泌腺 | B |
| endogenous | 内因性の⟷ exogenous | J |
| endomorphy | 内胚葉型 | G |
| enlightenment | 悟り | J |
| environment | 環境 | |
| envy | 羨望 | J |
| epidemiology | 疫学 | A |
| epigenesis | 後成説,漸成説 | A |
| epilepsy | てんかん | B J |
| episodic memory | エピソード記憶 | D |
| EPQ | =Eysenck Personality Questionaire | |
| equity | 衡平,公平 | I |
| equivalent stimulus | 等価刺激 | B |
| ergonomics | 人間工学→ human engineering | B |
| ERP | = event-related potential | |
| Es（独） | エス =id | J |
| ethical principles | 倫理綱領 | A |
| ethology | 比較行動学,行動生物学,動物行動学 | |
| event-related potential (ERP) | 事象関連電位 | B |
| evidence-based psychotherapy | 実証に基づく心理療法 | J |
| evoked potential | 誘発電位 | B C |
| excitation transfer theory | 興奮転移理論 | F I |
| exemplification | 示範 | I |
| existential analysis | 現存在分析（実存分析） | J |
| exogenous | 外因性の⟷ endogenous | J |

| expected value | 期待値 | K |
| --- | --- | --- |
| experience | 経験 | |
| experiencing | 体験過程 | J |
| experiment | 実験 | K |
| experimental condition | 実験条件 | K |
| experimental design | 実験計画法 | K |
| experimental group | 実験群 | K |
| experimenter | 実験者 | K |
| experimenter effect | 実験者効果 | K |
| explicit memory | 顕在記憶 | D |
| exploratory behavior | 探索行動 | H |
| expression | 表出，表現 | |
| external criterion | 外的基準 | K |
| externalization | 外在化⟷ internalization | H I J |
| extinction | 消去 | C |
| extraneous variable | 剰余変数 | K |
| extrapunitive response | 外罰的反応 | G J |
| extraversion | 外向性⟷ introversion | G |
| extrinsic motivation | 外発的動機づけ⟷ intrinsic motivation | F H |
| eye contact | アイコンタクト，視線の交錯 | E J |
| eye movement | 眼球運動 | B |
| Eysenck Personality Questionnaire (EPQ) | アイゼンク性格検査→ Maudsley Personality Inventory | G |

## F

| $F$ test | $F$ 検定 | K |
| --- | --- | --- |
| face recognition | 顔認識 | D |
| face sheet | フェイスシート | K |
| facial expression | 表情 | |
| facilitation | 促進，ファシリテーション | J |

| | | |
|---|---|---|
| factor | 要因 | |
| | 因子 | K |
| factor analysis | 因子分析 | K |
| factorial design | 要因計画 | K |
| fairy tale | おとぎ話 | |
| fantasy | 空想→ phantasy | H J |
| FAP | = fixed action pattern | |
| fashion | 流行 | I |
| fatherhood | 父性→ paternity | A H J |
| fatigue | 疲労 | B |
| fear | 恐怖, 不安 | F J |
| fear of stranger | 人見知り→ stranger anxiety | H J |
| fear-arousing communication | 恐怖喚起コミュニケーション | E |
| Fechner's law | フェヒナーの法則 | B |
| feedback | フィードバック | B D |
| feeding center | 摂食中枢 | B |
| feeding centre（英） | = feeding center | |
| feeling-as-information | 感情情報機能説 | F I |
| feminist therapy | フェミニスト・セラピー | J |
| fetal period | 胎児期 | A H |
| field | 場 | I |
| | 野, 領域 | B |
| field dependence | 場依存性 | I |
| field experiment | フィールド実験, 野外実験, 現場実験 | K |
| field theory | 場理論 | A |
| figural after-effect | 図形残効 | B |
| figure and ground | 図と地 | B |
| figure-ground | = figure and ground | |
| finger painting | フィンガーペインティング | J |
| finger sucking | 指しゃぶり | |

| | | |
|---|---|---|
| fitness | 適応度 | C |
| fixation | 凝視, 固着 | G J |
| fixed action pattern (FAP) | 固定的活動型, 固定的運動型, 固定的動作パターン | C |
| fixed interval (FI) reinforcement | 定間隔強化 | C |
| fixed ratio (FR) schedule | 定率強化スケジュール | C |
| floor effect | 床効果 | K |
| fluid intelligence | 流動性知能 | G |
| focusing | フォーカシング | J |
| folktale | 民話 | |
| follow-up | フォローアップ | J |
| footedness | 利き足 | B |
| foot-in-the-door technique | 段階的要請法 | I |
| forced choice | 強制選択 | K |
| forgetting | 忘却 | D |
| form perception | 形の知覚 | B |
| formal group | 公式集団, フォーマル・グループ ⟷ informal group | I |
| fovea | 中心窩 | B |
| frame of reference | 参照枠, 準拠枠 | B D E I |
| fraternal twins | 二卵性双生児 | |
| free association | 自由連想 | J |
| free recall | 自由再生 | D |
| free school | フリースクール | H |
| free-floating attention | 平等にただよう注意 | J |
| frequency | 頻度, 度数 | K |
| frequency distribution | 度数分布 | K |
| frequency of occurrence | 出現頻度 | E |
| frontal association area | 前頭連合野 | B |
| frontal lobe | 前頭葉 | B |

| | | |
|---|---|---|
| frustration | 欲求不満，フラストレーション | FGHJ |
| frustration tolerance | 欲求不満耐性 | F |
| functional autonomy | 機能的自律性 | FJ |
| functional disorder | 機能障害 | J |
| functionalism | 機能主義 | A |

## G

| | | |
|---|---|---|
| gain from illness | 疾病利得 | J |
| galvanic skin reflex (GSR) | = galvanic skin response | |
| galvanic skin response (GSR) | 皮膚電気反応<br>→ electrodermal response | B |
| gambler's fallacy | ギャンブラーの誤謬 | I |
| game analysis | ゲーム分析 | J |
| gang age | ギャングエイジ | AHI |
| ganglion | 神経節 | B |
| Gauss distribution | ガウス分布（正規分布） | K |
| gaze aversion | 視線回避 | J |
| gender | 心理社会的性，ジェンダー | |
| gender identity disorder | 性同一性障害 | J |
| gene | 遺伝子 | |
| generalization | 般化 | C |
| generation boundary | 世代間境界 | J |
| generative grammar | 生成文法 | E |
| genetic | 遺伝の，遺伝に関する | |
| genetic epistemology | 発生認識論 | AH |
| genital phase | 性器期 | GHJ |
| genital stage | = genital phase | |
| genogram | ジェノグラム，家系図 | J |
| genotype | 遺伝子型 ⟷ phenotype | AB |
| geographical environment | 地理的環境 | |

# geometrical illusion

| | | |
|---|---|---|
| geometrical illusion | 幾何学的錯視 | B |
| gerontology | 老年学 | A H |
| Gestalt（独） | ゲシュタルト | A |
| gesture | ジェスチャー | E |
| Gilles de la Tourette's syndrome | ジル・ド・ラ・トゥレット症候群→ Tourette's disorder | J |
| goal | 目標 | C F |
| goal directed behavior | 目標指向行動 | C F |
| goal gradient | 目標勾配 | C F |
| good enough mother | ほどよい母親 | H J |
| Goodenough Draw-a-Man test | グッドイナフ・テスト→ Draw-a-Man test | G J |
| good-poor analysis (G-P analysis) | 上位―下位分析，G-P 分析 | K |
| G-P analysis | = good-poor analysis | |
| grammar | 文法 | |
| graph theory | グラフ理論 | K |
| grasping reflex | 把握反射 | H |
| group | 群 | K |
| group dynamics | 集団力学，グループ・ダイナミクス | A |
| group norm | 集団規範 | I |
| group polarization | 集団成極化 | I |
| group supervision | グループ・スーパービジョン | J |
| growth | 成長 | H |
| growth model | 成長モデル | H K |
| GSR | = galvanic skin response | |
| guess-who test | ゲス・フー・テスト | G |
| guidance | 指導，ガイダンス | H |
| gustation | 味覚→ gustatory sense, sense of taste | B |
| gustatory sense | 味覚→ gustation, sense of taste | B |

## H

| | | |
|---|---|---|
| habit | 習慣 | C I |
| habit disorder | 習癖性障害 | J |
| habit strength | 習慣強度 | C |
| habituation | 慣れ，馴化 | C |
| hallucination | 幻覚 | J |
| halo effect | ハロー効果 | D I |
| handedness | 利き手 | B |
| Hawthorne study | ホーソン研究 | I |
| head banging | 頭部叩き | J |
| head control | 頸定(けいてい) | B J |
| healing | 癒(いや)し | J |
| health psychology | 健康心理学 | |
| hearing impairment | 聴力障害 | J |
| hebephrenia | 破瓜(はか)型統合失調症（破瓜病） | J |
| helping behavior | 援助行動 | H I J |
| helplessness | 無力感 → apathy | B C F J |
| hemiplegia | 片麻痺(へんまひ) | J |
| here and now | 今ここ | J |
| heredity | 遺伝 | |
| heuristic | ヒューリスティック | D |
| hierarchy of needs | 欲求階層（説） | F |
| high risk infant | ハイリスク乳幼児 | J |
| higher brain function | 高次脳機能 | B |
| high-functioning autism | 高機能自閉症 | J |
| hippocampus | 海馬 | B |
| HIV | = Human Immunodeficiency Virus | |
| holding | 抱っこ，ホールディング | H J |
| holism | 全体論 | A |
| homeostasis | ホメオスタシス，恒常状態 | B C F |

# homology

| | | |
|---|---|---|
| homology | 相同 ←→ analogy | B |
| homosexuality | 同性愛 | J |
| hospice | ホスピス | J |
| hospitalism | ホスピタリズム，施設病 | H J |
| hostility | 敵意 | |
| House-Tree-Person Test (HTP) | HTP テスト | G J |
| House-Tree-Person-Person Test (HTPP) | HTPP テスト | G J |
| HTP | =House-Tree-Person Test | |
| HTPP | =House-Tree-Person-Person Test | |
| human beings | 人類，（生物としての）ヒト | A B |
| human engineering | 人間工学 → ergonomics | B |
| Human Immunodeficiency Virus (HIV) | ヒト免疫不全ウィルス | B J |
| human resources management | 人的資源管理 | I |
| humanistic psychology | 人間性心理学 | |
| humor | ユーモア<br>体液 | G |
| humour（英） | = humor | |
| hypersomnia | 過眠（症） | J |
| hypertonia | 筋緊張亢進 | B J |
| hyperventilation syndrome | 過換気症候群 | J |
| hypnosis | 催眠 | B J |
| hypnotherapy | 催眠療法 | J |
| hypochondriasis | 心気症 | J |
| hypothalamus | 視床下部 | B |
| hypothesis | 仮説 → assumption | K |
| hypothesis testing | 仮説検証 | K |
| hysteria | ヒステリー | J |
| hysterical personality | ヒステリー性人格 | J |

## I

| | | |
|---|---|---|
| iatrogenic disease | 医原性疾患（医原病） | J |
| ICD | =International Classificantion of Diseases | |
| id | イド＝Es | J |
| idealization | 理想化 | J |
| identical twins | 一卵性双生児 | |
| identification | 同一化，同一視 | D H J |
| identified patient (IP) | 患者とみなされた者，指標となる患者 | J |
| identity | アイデンティティ，同一性 | G H |
| identity crisis | 同一性危機 | H |
| identity diffusion | 同一性拡散 | H J |
| identity disorder | 同一性障害 | J |
| ideogram | 表意文字 | E |
| idiographic method | 個性記述的研究 | K |
| Illinois Test of Psycholinguistic Abilities (ITPA) | イリノイ心理言語能力テスト | E J |
| illusion | 錯覚 | B |
| image | イメージ | |
| imagination | 想像 | B D G J |
| imitation | 模倣 | C H |
| impairment | 機能障害 | J |
| implicit memory | 潜在記憶 | D |
| implicit personality theory | 暗黙のパーソナリティ観 | I |
| impression formation | 印象形成 | I |
| imprinting | インプリンティング，刷り込み | C H |
| impulse | 衝動 | |
| impulsive behavior | 衝動行動 | J |
| impunitive response | 無罰的反応 | G J |

## inattention

| | | |
|---|---|---|
| inattention | 注意集中困難 | J |
| incentive | 誘因 | B C F |
| incest | 近親姦 | J |
| incidental learning | 偶発学習 | C |
| inclusion | インクルージョン，侵入 | J |
| inclusive fitness | 包括的適応度 | A B |
| incoherence | 思考散乱，支離滅裂 | J |
| incongruence | 不一致，不適合，不調和 | F G |
| incoordination | 協調運動障害 | J |
| independence | 独立，自立 | H |
| independent self | 相互独立的自己観 | I |
| independent variable | 独立変数 | K |
| individual differences | 個人差 | |
| individual unconscious | 個人的無意識 | J |
| individuation process | 個性化過程 | J |
| induced movement | 誘導運動 | B |
| induction | 帰納，帰納法⟵→ deduction<br>誘導，感応<br>感応 | B D<br>J |
| inductive thinking | 帰納的思考 | D |
| industrial counseling | 産業カウンセリング | I J |
| infancy | 乳児期 | A H |
| infantile sexuality | 幼児性欲 | J |
| infantilism | 幼稚症 | J |
| inference | 推論→ reasoning | D |
| inferiority complex | 劣等コンプレックス<br>⟵→ superiority complex | J |
| inferiority feeling | 劣等感 | F G H |
| informal group | インフォーマル・グループ，非公式集団⟵→ formal group | I |
| information processing | 情報処理 | D |

| | | |
|---|---|---|
| informational influence | 情報的影響 | I |
| informed consent | インフォームド・コンセント，説明による同意 | A K |
| ingratiation | 迎合，取り入り，追従 | I |
| in-group favoritism | 内集団びいき | I |
| in-group favouritism（英） | = in-group favoritism | |
| inhibit | 制止する，抑制する→ suppress | B F J |
| inhibition | 抑制，制止，禁止→ suppression | B F J |
| initial spurt | 初頭努力 | C |
| initiation | イニシエーション | J |
| ink-blot | インクブロット | G J |
| innate behavior | 生得的行動 | C |
| inner speech | 内言，内的言語，内語，内言語 | D E |
| inoculation theory | 接種理論 | I |
| input | 入力 | B C K |
| insight | 見通し，洞察 | D J |
| insight into disease | 病識 | J |
| insomnia | 不眠症 | J |
| instinct | 本能 | |
| instinctive behavior | 本能行動 | B C F |
| instruct | 教示する | K |
| instruction | 教授 | C |
| | 教示 | C K |
| instrumental conditioning | 道具的条件づけ | C |
| intake interview | インテーク面接，初回面接，受理面接 | J |
| integrate | 統合する | H J |
| integration | 統合教育 | H |
| intellectual disability | 知的障害 | H J |
| intellectualization | 知性化 | J |
| intelligence | 知能 | |

## intelligence quotient

| | | |
|---|---|---|
| intelligence quotient (IQ) | 知能指数 | G H J |
| intelligence test | 知能検査→ IQ test | G H J |
| intention | 意図, 志向 | D E |
| interaction | 交互作用, 相互作用 | H K |
| interaction effect | 交互作用効果 | K |
| interdependency | 相互依存性 | J |
| interdependent self | 相互協調的自己感 | I |
| interest | 興味, 関心 | |
| interindividual | 個人間の⟷ intraindividual<br>→ interpersonal | K |
| intermittent reinforcement | 間欠強化 | C |
| internal consistency | 内的整合性 | K |
| internal inhibition | 内制止 | C |
| internal secretion | 内分泌 | B |
| internal sense | 内部感覚 | B |
| internal validity | 内的妥当性 | K |
| internal working model (IWM) | 内的作業モデル | H J |
| internalization | 内在化⟷ externalization | H I J |
| International Classification of Diseases (ICD) | 国際疾病分類 | A J |
| interpersonal | 対人的な, 個人間の⟷ intrapersonal<br>→ interindividual | |
| interpersonal attraction | 対人魅力 | I |
| interpersonal cognition | 対人認知 | I |
| interpersonal relations | 対人関係 | |
| interpersonal theory | 対人関係論 | J |
| interpretation | 解釈 | J |
| intersubjectivity | 間主観性 | A J |
| interval scale | 間隔尺度 | K |
| intervening variable | 仲介変数→ mediating variable | K |

| | | |
|---|---|---|
| intervention | 介入 | J |
| interview | 面接 | K |
| intimacy | 親密さ | I J |
| intraindividual | 個人内の ⟷ interindividual<br>→ intrapersonal | K |
| intrapersonal | 個人内の ⟷ interpersonal<br>→ intraindividual | |
| intrinsic motivation | 内発的動機づけ<br>⟷ extrinsic motivation | F H |
| introjection | 取り入れ，取り込み | J |
| intropunitive response | 内罰的反応 | G J |
| introspection | 内観 | J |
| introversion | 内向性 ⟷ extraversion | G |
| inventory | 目録 | K |
| IP | = identified patient | |
| IQ | = intelligence quotient | |
| IQ score | IQ 得点 | G H J |
| IQ test | 知能検査 | G H J |
| isolation | 隔離，孤立 | |
| isomorphism | 同型論 | A |
| item analysis | 項目分析 | K |
| item response theory | 項目反応理論 | K |
| ITPA | = Illinois Test of Psycholinguistic Abilities | |
| IWM | = internal working model | |

| **J** | | |
|---|---|---|
| jealousy | 嫉妬 | H J |
| joint attention | 共同注視，共同注意，ジョイント・アテンション | E H |

## just noticeable difference

| just noticeable difference | 丁度可知差異，弁別閾→ differential limen, difference threshold, discriminative threshold | B |
| --- | --- | --- |
| juvenile delinquency | 少年非行 | |
| juvenile seclusion | 思春期内閉症 | J |

### K

| key stimulus | 鍵刺激 | B C |
| --- | --- | --- |
| key-person | キーパーソン | J |
| KFD | = kinetic family drawings | |
| kinaesthesia（英） | = kinesthesia | |
| kinaesthesis（英） | = kinesthesis | |
| kinesiology | 運動学 | |
| kinesthesia | 運動感覚 | B |
| kinesthesis | = kinesthesia | |
| kinetic family drawings (KFD) | 動的家族描画法 | G |
| knowledge | 知識 | |

### L

| labeling | ラベリング，レッテル貼り | D H J |
| --- | --- | --- |
| labelling（英） | = labeling | |
| laboratory | 実験室 | K |
| landscape montage technique | 風景構成法 | J |
| language | 言語 | |
| language acquisition | 言語獲得 | E H J |
| latency | 潜時 | C |
| latency period | 潜伏期 | G H J |
| latent learning | 潜在学習 | C |
| lateralization | 側性化 | B |
| LD | = learning disorder, learning disability | |

| | | |
|---|---|---|
| leadership | リーダーシップ | I |
| learn | 学習する | |
| learned helplessness | 学習性無力感 | C J |
| learning | 学習 | |
| learning curve | 学習曲線 | C |
| learning disability (LD) | 学習障害→ learning disorder | H J |
| learning disorder (LD) | 学習障害→ learning disability | H J |
| learning set | 学習の構え | C |
| least significant difference (*LSD*) | 最小有意差 | K |
| level | 水準 | |
| level of aspiration | 要求水準 | |
| level of psychopathology | 病態水準 | J |
| level of significance | 有意水準 | K |
| libido | リビドー（論） | J |
| lie scale | 虚偽尺度 | K |
| life history | 生活史, 生育史, 生活歴 | H J |
| life-span development | 生涯発達 | H |
| light adaptation | 明順応 | B |
| light and dark adaptation | 明暗順応 | B |
| lightness | 明るさ | |
| Likert scale | リカート尺度 | K |
| limbic system | 大脳辺縁系 | B |
| limen | 閾→ threshold | B |
| limited interest | 限局的興味 | J |
| literacy | リテラシー | |
| localization | 局在（化）, 定位 | |
| localization theory | 機能局在論 | B |
| locus of control | ローカス・オブ・コントロール, 統制の所在 | D G I |
| longitudinal study | 縦断的研究 | H K |

| | | |
|---|---|---|
| long-term memory | 長期記憶 | B D |
| looking-glass self | 鏡映的自己 | G H J |
| low-ball technique | 承諾先取り法 | I |
| *LSD* | = least significant difference | |
| luminance | 輝度 | B |

## M

| | | |
|---|---|---|
| *M* | = mean | |
| MA | = mental age | |
| Machiavellian intelligence | マキャベリ的知能 | B G I |
| macroscopic behavior | 巨視的行動<br>⟷ microscopic behavior<br>→ molar behavior | C D |
| magnetic resonance imaging (MRI) | 磁気共鳴画像 | B |
| magnetoencephalogram (MEG) | 脳磁図 | B |
| main effect | 主効果 | K |
| majority | 多数者,マジョリティ ⟷ minority | I |
| maladjustment | 不適応 | J |
| manic defense | 躁的防衛 | J |
| man-machine system | 人間―機械系 | I |
| MANOVA | = multivariate analysis of variance | |
| marginal man | 境界人, 周辺人 | H I |
| marital counseling | 夫婦カウンセリング | J |
| Markov chain | マルコフ連鎖 | K |
| marriage counseling | 結婚カウンセリング | J |
| masculinity-femininity scale | 性度検査 | G J |
| masking | マスキング | B |
| masking effect | 遮断効果 | B |
| masochism | マゾヒズム ⟷ sadism | J |

| | | |
|---|---|---|
| maternal deprivation | 母性剥奪, マターナル・ディプリベーション | H J |
| maternal separation | 母子分離 | H J |
| maternity | 母性→ motherhood | A H J |
| maturation | 成熟 | H |
| Maudsley Personality Inventory (MPI) | モーズレイ性格検査→ Eysenck Personality Questionnaire | G |
| maximum likelihood estimate method | 最尤推定法 | K |
| maximum likelihood estimation method | = maximum likelihood estimate method | |
| maze | 迷路 | C D |
| MBD | = Minimal Brain Dysfunction | |
| MDS | = multidimensional scaling | |
| mean ($M$) | 平均値→ average | K |
| measure | 測度 | K |
| measurement | 測定 | K |
| media literacy | メディアリテラシー | |
| median | 中央値, メディアン | K |
| mediating variable | 媒介変数→ intervening variable | K |
| meditation | 瞑想 | J |
| MEG | = magnetoencephalogram | |
| melancholia | メランコリー, うつ病 | J |
| melancholic type | メランコリー親和型性格 | J |
| memorization | 記銘 | D |
| memory | 記憶 | B D |
| memory span | 記憶範囲, 記憶容量 | B D |
| mental age (MA) | 精神年齢 | G H J |
| mental disorder | 精神障害 | H J |
| mental effort | 心的努力 | D |
| mental health | 精神衛生 | |

| | | |
|---|---|---|
| mental imagery | 心的イメージ | D |
| mental retardation | 精神遅滞 | G H J |
| mental rotation | 心的回転 | C D |
| mental saturation | 心的飽和 | B D |
| mesomorphy | 中胚葉型 | G |
| meta-analysis | メタ分析 | K |
| metacognition | メタ認知 | D |
| metamemory | メタ記憶 | D |
| metaphor | 隠喩(いんゆ) | D E |
| methamphetamine | メタアンフェタミン→ amphetamine | B |
| method | 方法 | K |
| method of adjustment | 調整法 | K |
| method of constant stimuli | 恒常法，恒常刺激法→ constant method | K |
| method of equal-appearing intervals | 等現間隔法 | K |
| method of limits | 極限法 | K |
| method of magnitude estimation | マグニチュード推定法 | K |
| method of paired comparisons | 一対比較法 | K |
| method of rank order | 順位法 | K |
| micrographia | 小字症 | J |
| micropsia | 小視症 | J |
| microscopic behavior | 微視的行動 ⟷ macroscopic behavior → molecular behavior | C D |
| middle childhood | 児童期 | A H |
| migraine | 偏頭痛 | B |
| milestone | 里程標 | |
| milieu therapy | 環境療法 | J |

| | | |
|---|---|---|
| mind-body correlation | 心身相関 | J |
| Minimal Brain Dysfunction (MBD) | 微細脳機能障害 | B J |
| Minnesota Multiphasic Personality Inventory (MMPI) | ミネソタ多面人格目録 | G |
| minor anomaly | 小奇形 | J |
| minority | 少数者，マイノリティ<br>⟷ majority | I |
| mirror drawing | 鏡映描写 | B |
| misdiagnosis | 誤診 | J |
| missing value | 欠損値 | K |
| MMPI | =Minnesota Multiphasic Personality Inventory | |
| mob | モッブ，乱衆 | I |
| modality | 感覚モダリティ，モダリティ→<br>sense modality | B |
| mode | 最頻値，モード | K |
| modeling | モデリング | C H |
| modelling (英) | = modeling | |
| modularity | モジュラリティ | D |
| molar behavior | モル的行動，総体的行動<br>⟷ molecular behavior<br>→ macroscopic behavior | C D |
| molecular behavior | 分子的行動<br>⟷ molar behavior<br>→ microscopic behavior | C D |
| mood | 気分 | F |
| mood-congruent memory | 気分一致記憶 | D |
| mood-dependent memory | 気分依存記憶 | D |
| moon illusion | 月の錯視 | B |
| moral | 道徳，道徳性 | |
| morale | モラール，士気，目標達成への意欲 | F I |

| | | |
|---|---|---|
| moratorium | モラトリアム | H I J |
| Morgan's Canon | モーガンの公準 | A |
| Moro reflex | モロー反射 | B H |
| mother-child relationship | 母子関係 | |
| motherese | 母親語，マザリーズ | E H |
| motherhood | 母性→ maternity | A H J |
| mother-infant fixation | 母子固着 | H J |
| mother-infant interaction | 母子相互作用 | B H |
| mothering | マザリング | H |
| motion perception | 運動の知覚 | B |
| motivation | 動機づけ | |
| motive | 動機 | F |
| motor clumsiness | 運動の不器用さ | B J |
| motor control | 運動制御 | B |
| motor learning | 運動学習 | C |
| motor skill | 運動技能 | |
| mourning work | 喪の仕事 | J |
| MPI | = Maudsley Personality Inventory | |
| MRI | = magnetic resonance imaging | |
| multicollinearity | 多重共線性 | K |
| multidimensional scaling (MDS) | 多次元尺度構成法 | K |
| multiple choice | 多肢選択 | K |
| multiple comparison | 多重比較 | K |
| multiple correlation | 重相関 | K |
| multiple correlation coefficient | 重相関係数 | K |
| multiple personality | 多重人格 | J |
| multiple regression analysis | 重回帰分析 | K |
| multivariate analysis | 多変量解析 | K |

| | | |
|---|---|---|
| multivariate analysis of variance (MANOVA) | 多変量分散分析 | K |
| muscle strength | 筋力 | B |
| muscle tone | 筋緊張 | B |
| music therapy | 音楽療法 | J |
| mutism | 緘黙（症） | J |
| myth | 神話 | A J |

### N

| | | |
|---|---|---|
| NA | = noradrenaline | |
| nail biting | 爪かみ（症） | J |
| naive participant | ナイーブな参加者⟷ confederate | K |
| naive theory | 素朴理論 | D H |
| narcissism | 自己愛，ナルシシズム | G J |
| narcissistic personality disorder | 自己愛人格障害 | J |
| narcolepsy | ナルコレプシー | J |
| national character | 国民性 | A I |
| native language | 母語 | E |
| nativism | 生得論 | A H |
| natural language processing | 自然言語処理 | E |
| natural selection | 自然淘汰，自然選択 | A |
| naturalistic observation | 自然観察 | K |
| nature | 生得的性質 | A H |
| nature or nurture | 氏か育ちか | A H |
| NE | = norepinephrine | |
| near death experience | 臨死体験 | J |
| need | 要求，欲求 | |
| negative | 負の⟷ positive | K |
| negative emotion | 否定的感情⟷ positive emotion | F J |
| negative transference | 陰性転移⟷ positive transference | J |

| negativism | 反抗症，拒絶症 | J |
| --- | --- | --- |
| neo-behaviorism | 新行動主義 | A |
| neonate | 新生児→ newborn child | A B H |
| nervous system | 神経系 | B |
| neural network | ニューラル・ネットワーク | B D |
| neuron | ニューロン | B |
| neuropsychology | 神経心理学 | |
| neurosis | 神経症 | J |
| neurotransmitter | 神経伝達物質 | B |
| neutrality | 中立性 | J |
| newborn child | 新生児→ neonate | A H |
| night terror | 夜驚→ sleep terror, nightmare | J |
| night walking | 夜間徘徊 | J |
| nightmare | 夜驚，悪夢→<br>　night terror, sleep terror | J |
| nocturnal enuresis | 夜尿症 | J |
| nominal scale | 名義尺度 | K |
| non-attendance at school | 不登校 | H J |
| non-directive counseling | 非指示的カウンセリング | J |
| nonparametric method | ノンパラメトリック法 | K |
| nonparametric test | ノンパラメトリック検定法→<br>　nonparametric method | K |
| non-rapid eye movement（non-REM） | 非急速眼球運動，ノンレム | B |
| non-rapid eye movement sleep（NREM sleep） | ノンレム睡眠 | B |
| non-REM | = non-rapid eye movement | |
| non-verbal | 非言語的，非言語性（の） | E G |
| non-verbal communication（NVC） | ノンバーバル・コミュニケーション，<br>　非言語的コミュニケーション | |
| noradrenalin | = noradrenaline | |
| noradrenaline（NA） | ノルアドレナリン→ norepinephrine | B |

| | | |
|---|---|---|
| norepinephrine (NE) | ノルエピネフリン→ noradrenaline | B |
| normal distribution | 正規分布 | K |
| normalization | ノーマリゼーション | J K |
| NREM sleep | = non-rapid eye movement sleep | |
| nuclear family | 核家族 | |
| null hypothesis | 帰無仮説 | K |
| nurture | 養育→ parenting | B H |
| nutrition | 栄養摂取 | |
| NVC | = non-verbal communication | E |

## O

| | | |
|---|---|---|
| obedience | 服従 | I |
| obesity | 肥満症 | J |
| object constancy | 対象恒常性 | B C F |
| object loss | 対象喪失 | J |
| objective | 客観的な⟷ subjective | |
| observation | 観察 | B K |
| observational learning | 観察学習 | C |
| observe | 観察する | |
| obsession | 強迫観念 | J |
| obsessional neurosis | 強迫神経症 | J |
| obsessive | 強迫的,強迫性の→ compulsive | J |
| obsessive-compulsive disorder (OCD) | 強迫性障害,強迫症 | J |
| occupational therapy (OT) | 作業療法 | J |
| OCD | = obsessive-compulsive disorder | |
| Oedipal phase | エディプス期 | J |
| Oedipus complex | エディプス・コンプレックス | G J |
| olfaction | 嗅覚→ olfactory sense, sense of smell | B |
| olfactory sense | 嗅覚→ olfaction, sense of smell | B |
| one-way layout | 一元配置 | K |

| | | |
|---|---|---|
| one-way mirror | 一方向鏡，マジック・ミラー | K |
| ontogenesis | = ontogeny | |
| ontogeny | 個体発生 ⟷ phylogeny | A B H |
| open school | オープンスクール | H J |
| operant conditioning | オペラント条件づけ | C |
| operate | 機能する | C D |
| operational definition | 操作的定義 | K |
| operationalism | 操作主義 → operationism | A |
| operationism | 操作主義 → operationalism | A |
| opinion leader | オピニオン・リーダー | I |
| oppositional defiant disorder | 反抗挑戦性障害 | J |
| optic chiasm | 視神経交叉(こうさ) | B |
| optic nerve | 視神経 | B |
| optimistic illusion | 楽観的な幻想 | J |
| optimization | 最適化 | H |
| oral phase | 口唇期(こうしんき) | G H J |
| ordinal scale | 順序尺度 | K |
| organic psychosis | 器質精神病 | J |
| organization | 体制化 | D |
| orientation | 見当識(けんとうしき) | B J |
| OT | = occupational therapy | |
| outsider | アウトサイダー | I |
| over-adjustment | 過剰適応 | J |

## P

| | | |
|---|---|---|
| panic | パニック | J |
| panic disorder | パニック障害 | J |
| paradigm | パラダイム | |
| parallel distributed processing | 並列分散処理 | D |
| parallel processing | 並列処理 | B D |

| | | |
|---|---|---|
| paranoia | 妄想症，パラノイア | J |
| paranoid-schizoid position | 妄想分裂ポジション，妄想分裂態勢 | J |
| parasympathetic nervous system (PNS) | 副交感神経系 | B |
| parent effectiveness training | 親業訓練 | H J |
| parent-child relationship | 親子関係 | |
| parenting | 養育→ nurture | H |
| parietal lobe | 頭頂葉 | B |
| partial correlation coefficient | 偏相関係数 | K |
| participant | （研究・調査への）参加者，協力者→ subject | K |
| participant observation | 関与しながらの観察<br>参与観察 | J<br>K |
| paternalism | 温情主義，父性的干渉主義 | A J |
| paternity | 父性→ fatherhood | A H J |
| path analysis | パス解析 | K |
| pathography | 病跡学 | J |
| PDD | = pervasive developmental disorder | |
| peer counseling | ピア・カウンセリング | J |
| penis envy | ペニス羨望 | J |
| perception | 知覚 | B |
| perceptual organization | 知覚的体制化 | B |
| performance intelligence | 動作性知能 | G |
| performance test | 作業検査，動作性検査 | G J |
| perinatal period | 周産期 | A B H |
| perseveration | 固執，保続 | J |
| persona | ペルソナ | J |
| personal communication | パーソナル・コミュニケーション | E |
| personal space | パーソナル・スペース，個人空間 | I |
| personality | 人格，パーソナリティ | G |
| personality disorder | 人格障害 | J |

## personality test

| | | |
|---|---|---|
| personality test | 性格検査，人格検査 | G |
| person-centered approach | パーソン・センタード・アプローチ，人間中心セラピー | J |
| perspective-taking | 他視点取得 | D |
| pervasive developmental disorder（PDD） | 広汎性発達障害 | H J |
| phallic phase | 男根期 | G H J |
| phantasy | 幻想，空想→ fantasy | J |
| phantom limb | 幻肢 | B |
| phenomenological psychology | 現象学的心理学 | |
| phenomenology | 現象学 | A |
| phenomenon of possession | 憑依現象 | J |
| phenotype | 表現型⟷ genotype | A B |
| phobia | 恐怖症 | J |
| phonogram | 表音文字 | E |
| phylogeny | 系統発生⟷ ontogeny | A B H |
| physical | 身体的な，物理的な | |
| physical therapy（PT） | 理学療法→ physiotherapy | J |
| physiotherapy | 理学療法→ physical therapy | J |
| pica | 異食 | J |
| Picture-Frustration Study | PF スタディ | F G J |
| placebo | プラシーボ，プラセボ，偽薬 | J |
| plasticity | 可塑性 | B |
| plateau phenomenon | 高原現象，プラトー現象 | A |
| play | 遊び | |
| play therapy | 遊戯療法 | J K |
| pleasure principle | 快楽原則 | J |
| PM theory | PM 理論 | I |
| PNS | = parasympathetic nervous system | |
| population | 母集団 | K |

| | | |
|---|---|---|
| position | ポジション，態勢 | J |
| positive | 正の⟵→ negative | K |
| positive emotion | 肯定的感情⟵→ negative emotion | F J |
| positive illusion | 肯定的幻想，ポジティブ・イリュージョン | J |
| positive transference | 陽性転移⟵→ negative transference | J |
| post hoc | 事後の⟵→ prior | K |
| post-event information effect | 事後情報効果 | D |
| post-traumatic stress disorder (PTSD) | （心的）外傷後ストレス障害 | J |
| postural tremor | 姿勢（時）振戦 | J |
| pragmatic dysfunction | 語用機能障害 | J |
| pragmatic function | 語用機能 | C E |
| preceding study | 先行研究 | K |
| preconscious | 前意識（の） | G J |
| prediction | 予測 | |
| predictive validity | 予測的妥当性 | K |
| prefrontal cortex | 前頭前野 | B |
| prejudice | 偏見 | I |
| premature infant | 未熟児 | B H J |
| premenstrual syndrome | 月経前症候群 | B |
| premorbid | 病前の | J |
| prenatal period | 出生前期 | A H B |
| pretend play | ごっこ遊び，ふり遊び | H |
| prevalence | 有病率 | J |
| primacy effect | 初頭効果 | C D I |
| primal scene | 原光景 | J |
| primary care | プライマリ・ケア | H |
| priming | プライミング | D |
| primitive defense mechanism | 原始的防衛機制 | J |
| primitive idealization | 原始的理想化 | J |

## principal component analysis

| | | |
|---|---|---|
| principal component analysis | 主成分分析 | K |
| prior | 事前の ⟵⟶ post hoc | K |
| private speech | 私的発話 | E |
| proactive inhibition | 順向抑制 ⟵⟶ retroactive inhibition | C D |
| probability | 確率 | K |
| probability judgment | 確率的判断 | K |
| problem solving | 問題解決 | D |
| problematic behavior | 問題行動 | H J |
| procedural justice | 手続的公正 | I |
| procedural knowledge | 手続的知識 | D |
| procedural memory | 手続記憶 | D |
| procedure | 手続き | K |
| process of therapy | 治療過程 | J |
| process scale | 過程尺度 | J |
| processing resource | 処理資源 | D |
| profile | プロフィール | |
| prognosis | 予後 | J |
| projection | 投影,投射 | J |
| projective identification | 投影性同一視 | J |
| projective technique | 投影法,投映法 | K |
| promax rotation | プロマックス回転 | K |
| proposition | 命題 | A E |
| propositional representation | 命題表象 | D |
| prospect theory | プロスペクト理論 | D I |
| prospective memory | 展望的記憶 | D |
| prospective study | 前方視的研究 | K |
| protocol | プロトコル | J |
| proximal stimulus | 近刺激 ⟵⟶ distal stimulus | B |
| pseudo | 仮性の,擬似の | J |
| psychiatrist | 精神科医 | |

| psychic energy | 心的エネルギー | J |
| --- | --- | --- |
| psychic trauma | 心的外傷 | J |
| psychoanalysis | 精神分析 | A J K |
| psychodynamics | 精神力動（論） | J |
| psychoeducation | 心理教育 | A |
| psychogenic | 心因の | J |
| psychogenic reaction | 心因性反応 | J |
| psycholinguistics | 心理言語学 | |
| psychological assessment | 心理査定，心理診断，心理アセスメント | G J |
| psychological test | 心理テスト | K |
| psychologist | 心理学者 | |
| psychopathology | 精神病理（学） | J |
| psychopathy | 精神病質 | J |
| psychophysical methods | 精神物理学的測定法 | B |
| psychophysics | 精神物理学，心理物理学 | |
| psychosis | 精神病 | J |
| psycho-social crisis | 心理社会的危機 | H J |
| psychosomatic disease | 心身症 | B J |
| psychotherapist | 心理療法士，サイコセラピスト | |
| psychotherapy | 心理療法，精神療法 | J K |
| PT | = physical therapy | |
| PTSD | = post-traumatic stress disorder | |
| puberty | 思春期 | A H |
| pupil | 瞳孔(どうこう) | B |
| purpose | （研究）目的→ aim | K |
| Pygmalion effect | ピグマリオン効果 | D H |

## Q

| QOL | = quality of life | |
| --- | --- | --- |

| quality of life (QOL) | 生活の質 | J |
| --- | --- | --- |
| quasi-experimental design | 準実験計画 | K |
| questionnaire | 質問紙 | K |

# R

| random sampling | ランダム抽出，無作為抽出 | K |
| --- | --- | --- |
| rank order correlation coefficient | 順位相関係数 | K |
| rapid eye movement (REM) | レム，急速眼球運動 | B |
| rapport | ラポール，ラポート | I J |
| rating method | 評定法 | K |
| rating scale | 評定尺度 | K |
| ratio scale | 比尺度，比例尺度 | K |
| rationalization | 合理化 | J |
| reaction | 反応→ response | |
| reaction formation | 反動形成 | J |
| reaction potential | 反応ポテンシャル | C D |
| reaction time | 反応時間 | C D |
| reactive psychosis | 反応性精神病 | J |
| reading | 読み | D |
| reality principle | 現実原則 | J |
| reality testing | 現実吟味，現実検討 | J |
| reasoning | 推論→ inference | D |
| recall | 再生 | D |
| recency effect | 新近効果，親近効果 | D |
| receptive field | 受容野 | B |
| receptor cell | 受容器 | B |
| reciprocal altruism | 互恵的利他主義 | I |
| recognition | 再認 | D |
| recreational therapy | リクリエーション療法 | J |

| | | |
|---|---|---|
| reference | 引用文献 | K |
| reference group | 準拠集団，レファレンス・グループ | I |
| reflex | 反射 | B C |
| reframing | リフレーミング | I J |
| regression | 退行 | H J |
| | 回帰 | K |
| regression analysis | 回帰分析 | K |
| rehabilitation | 社会復帰，リハビリテーション | J |
| reinforcement | 強化 | C |
| relative | 相対的な | K |
| relative evaluation | 相対評価 | K |
| relaxation | リラクセーション | J |
| reliability | 信頼性 | K |
| REM | = rapid eye movement | |
| remission | 寛解 | J |
| repeated measures analysis of variance | 反復測定のある分散分析 | K |
| repetition compulsion | 反復強迫 | J |
| representation | 表象 | D |
| repress | 抑圧する | J |
| repression | 抑圧 | J |
| residual | 残差 | K |
| resilience | 弾力性 | G H J |
| resistance | 抵抗 | I J |
| resource | 資源 | |
| respond | 反応する | |
| response | 反応→ reaction | B |
| restriction | 制限 | |
| result | 結果 | K |
| retina | 網膜 | B |
| retrieval | 検索 | D |

## retrieval cue

| | | |
|---|---|---|
| retrieval cue | 検索手がかり | D |
| retroactive inhibition | 逆向抑制 ⟵⟶ proactive inhibition | C D |
| retrospective memory | 回想的記憶 | D J |
| reward | 報酬 | C |
| rigidity | 硬さ | J |
| risk | リスク | H I J |
| role play | ロールプレイ | J |
| Rorschach Test | ロールシャッハ・テスト | G J |
| rumor | 流言 | I |
| rumour（英） | = rumor | |

## S

| | | |
|---|---|---|
| sadism | サディズム ⟵⟶ masochism | J |
| safety base | 安全基地 → secure base | H |
| sample | 標本，サンプル | K |
| sampling | = sample<br>標本抽出，サンプリング | K |
| sand play technique | 箱庭療法 | J |
| scaffolding | 足場（づくり） | C H |
| scale | 尺度 | K |
| scaling method | 尺度構成法 | K |
| scapegoat | スケープゴート，スケープゴート説 | I J |
| schema | スキーマ | B C D H |
| | シェマ | D H |
| schizophrenia | 統合失調症 | J |
| schizophrenic | 統合失調症の | J |
| school consultation | 学校コンサルテーション | J |
| school counselor | スクールカウンセラー | |
| school phobia | 登校恐怖症 | H J |
| school psychologist | 学校心理士，スクールサイコロジスト | |
| school refusal | 登校拒否 | H J |

| | | |
|---|---|---|
| school social work | スクール・ソーシャルワーク | H J |
| school violence | 校内暴力 | H J |
| scientist-practitioner model | 科学者―実践家モデル | J |
| scoring | 得点化, 採点, スコアリング | K |
| screening | スクリーニング, ふるい分け | K |
| screening test | スクリーニング・テスト | K |
| scribble | なぐり描き→ squiggle | J |
| script analysis | 脚本分析 | J |
| SCT | = Sentence Completion Test | |
| SD | = standard deviation<br>= semantic differential | |
| SDD | = specific developmental disorder | |
| second language | 第二言語 | E |
| secondary sex characteristics | 第二次性徴 | H |
| secure base | 安全基地→ safety base | H |
| selective attention | 選択的注意 | D |
| selective mutism | 場面緘黙(かんもく) | J |
| self | 自己 | |
| self control | 自己統制法 | B J |
| self help group | セルフヘルプ・グループ, 自助グループ | J |
| self psychology | 自己心理学 | |
| self-acceptance | 自己受容 | G J |
| self-actualization | 自己実現 | F G I J |
| self-analysis | 自己分析 | G J |
| self-awareness | 自己覚知, 自覚 | H I J |
| self-concept | 自己概念 | G H I J |
| self-consciousness | 自己意識 | |
| self-efficacy | 自己効力感, セルフ・エフィカシー | H J |
| self-enhancement | 自己高揚 | I |
| self-esteem | 自尊心, 自尊感情 | G I |

| | | |
|---|---|---|
| self-evaluation | 自己評価 | K |
| self-handicapping | セルフ・ハンディキャッピング | I |
| self-monitoring | セルフ・モニタリング | I |
| self-mutilation | 自傷 | J |
| self-presentation | 自己呈示（提示） | I |
| semantic differential (SD) | セマンティック・ディファレンシャル，意味微分 | K |
| semantic differential method | セマンティック・ディファレンシャル法，SD法，意味微分法 | K |
| semantic memory | 意味記憶 | D |
| semantic network | 意味ネットワーク | D |
| sensation | 感覚→ sense | B |
| sense | 感覚→ sensation | B |
| sense modality | 感覚モダリティ，モダリティ→ modality | B |
| sense of hearing | 聴覚→ audition，auditory sense | B |
| sense of sight | 視覚→ vision，visual sense | B |
| sense of smell | 嗅覚→ olfaction，olfactory sense | B |
| sense of taste | 味覚→ gustation，gustatory sense | B |
| sense of touch | 触角→ tactile sense | B |
| sensitivity training | 感受性訓練 | J |
| Sentence Completion Test (SCT) | 文章完成法テスト | G J |
| sentence comprehension | 文理解 | E |
| separation anxiety | 分離不安 | H J |
| separation-individuation theory | 分離―個体化理論 | A G H J |
| serial position effect | 系列位置効果 | C D |
| serotonin | セロトニン，5-HT | B |
| severe mental and physical disability | 重度心身障害 | J |
| sex counseling | セックス・カウンセリング | J |

| | | |
|---|---|---|
| sex role | 性役割 | I |
| sexual abuse | 性的虐待 | J |
| sexual dimorphism | 性的二型 | B |
| sexual drive theory | 性欲動論 | G J |
| sexual harassment | 性的ハラスメント | J |
| sexual perversion | 性的倒錯 | J |
| sexual trauma | 性的外傷 | J |
| shadow | 影 | J |
| shaman | シャーマン | A |
| shame | 恥 | |
| short-term memory | 短期記憶 | B D |
| siblings relationship | きょうだい関係 | H |
| sign | 記号 | D |
| sign test | サイン検定 | K |
| signal detection theory | 信号検出理論 | K |
| significant | （統計的に）有意な | K |
| significant others | 重要な他者，意味のある他者 | J |
| silence | 沈黙 | J |
| simple main effect | 単純主効果 | K |
| simulation | シミュレーション | D |
| single parent | シングル・ペアレント，単親 | H I |
| skill | 技能 | |
| sleep disorder | 睡眠障害 | J |
| sleep terror | 夜驚 → night terror, nightmare | J |
| sleep-walking | 夢中遊行症，夢遊病 | J |
| SNS | = sympathetic nervous system | |
| sociability | 社会性 | |
| social character | 社会的性格 | G I |
| social competence | 社会的コンピテンス | H |
| social constructivism | 社会構築主義 | A |

## social context

| | | |
|---|---|---|
| social context | 社会的文脈 | |
| social identity theory | 社会的アイデンティティ理論 | GI |
| social learning theory | 社会的学習理論 | HI |
| social norm | 社会的規範 | I |
| social reference | 社会的参照, ソーシャル・リファレンス | H |
| social skill | 社会的スキル, ソーシャル・スキル | CHI |
| social skill training (SST) | ソーシャル・スキルトレーニング | J |
| social support | ソーシャル・サポート | HIJ |
| social survey | 社会調査 | K |
| social value | 社会的価値 | I |
| social work | ソーシャルワーク | I |
| socialization | 社会化 | |
| sociodrama | ソシオドラマ | J |
| sociogram | ソシオグラム | HI |
| sociomatrix | ソシオマトリックス | HI |
| Sociometric Test | ソシオメトリック・テスト | HI |
| sociometry | ソシオメトリー | HI |
| sociopathy | 社会病質 | J |
| somatic sense | 体性感覚 | B |
| somatization disorder | 身体化障害 | J |
| somatognostic disorder | 身体認知障害 | J |
| sound localization | 音源定位 | B |
| source monitoring | ソース・モニタリング | D |
| space perception | 空間知覚 | B |
| span of attention | 注意の範囲 | D |
| special class | 特殊学級 | H |
| specific developmental disorder (SDD) | 特異的発達障害 | HJ |
| speech therapist (ST) | 言語療法士, スピーチ・セラピスト | |
| spiral of silence | 沈黙の螺旋(らせん) | I |

| | | |
|---|---|---|
| split brain | 分離脳 | B |
| splitting | 分裂 | J |
| spontaneous remission | 自然治癒力 | J |
| spreading activation | 活性化拡散 | D |
| squiggle | なぐり描き→ scribble | J |
| ST | = speech therapist | |
| SST | = social skill training | |
| stage fright | あがり | J |
| standard deviation ($SD$) | 標準偏差 | K |
| standardization | 標準化 | K |
| standardized | 標準化された | K |
| Stanford-Binet Intelligence test | スタンフォード・ビネー知能検査 | G |
| statistical power | 統計検定力, 検定力, 検出力 | K |
| step-wise selection | ステップワイズ変数選択 | K |
| stereopsis | 立体視→ stereoscopic vision | B |
| stereoscopic vision | 立体視→ stereopsis | B |
| stereotype | ステレオタイプ, 画一性 | G I |
| stereotypic action | 常同行為 | B J |
| stereotypic behavior | 常同的行動 | J |
| stereotypy | 常同症 | J |
| Stevens' law | スティーヴンスの法則 | B |
| stimulation | 刺激→ stimulus | B C |
| stimulus | 刺激→ stimulation | B |
| strange situation procedure | ストレンジ・シチュエーション法 | H K |
| stranger anxiety | 人見知り→ fear of stranger | H |
| strategy | 戦略, 方略 | |
| stress | ストレス | B C J |
| stressor | ストレッサー | B C J |
| stroke | ストローク | J |
| stroop test | ストループテスト | B |

# student counseling

| | | |
|---|---|---|
| student counseling | 学生相談 | H J |
| student guidance | 生徒指導 | H |
| stupor | 昏迷 | J |
| stuttering | 吃音(きつおん) | E J |
| subconscious | 下意識の | G J |
| subconsciousness | 下意識 | J |
| subculture | サブカルチャー | I |
| subject | 被験者→ participant | K |
| subjective | 主観的な ⟷ objective | |
| sublimation | 昇華 | G |
| subliminal perception | 閾下知覚(いきか) | B |
| subtest | 下位検査 | K |
| suggestion | 暗示 | J |
| suicide | 自殺 | J |
| superiority complex | 優越コンプレックス ⟷ inferiority complex | J |
| supervisee | スーパーバイジー | J |
| supervision | スーパービジョン | J |
| supervisor | スーパーバイザー | J |
| support | サポート，援助（する）<br>支持 | I<br>J |
| suppress | 抑制する→ inhibit | J |
| suppression | 抑制→ inhibition | J |
| symbiosis | 共生 | |
| symbol | 象徴 | |
| symbolic function | 象徴機能 | D H |
| sympathetic nervous system (SNS) | 交感神経系 | B |
| symptom | 症状 | |
| symptom formation | 症状形成 | J |
| synaesthesia（英） | = synesthesia | |

| | | |
|---|---|---|
| synaesthesis (英) | = synesthesis | |
| synapse | シナプス | B |
| synchronicity | 共時性 | J |
| syncope | 失神 | J |
| syndrome | 症候群, シンドローム | |
| syndrome shift | 症候移動 | J |
| synesthesia | 共感覚 | B |
| synesthesis | = synesthesia | |
| syntactic parsing | 統語解析 | E |
| syntax | 統語論 | E |
| systems approach | システムズ・アプローチ | J |
| Szondi Test | ソンディ・テスト | G J |

## T

| | | |
|---|---|---|
| tactile sense | 触覚→ sense of touch | B |
| target | 目標刺激 | D |
| TAT | =Thematic Apperception Test | |
| taxis | 走性 | B C |
| teacher counselor | 教師カウンセラー | H J |
| team teaching | チーム・ティーチング | H |
| telephone counseling | 電話相談 | J |
| temperament | 気質 | F G H |
| temporal lobe | 側頭葉 | B |
| territory | なわばり | C I |
| terror-management theory | 恐怖管理理論 | I |
| test | 検査（テスト）<br>検定 | K |
| test anxiety | テスト不安 | F |
| test battery | テストバッテリー→ battery | K |
| testee | = test taker | |

| | | |
|---|---|---|
| test of proportion | 比率の差の検定 | K |
| test report | 検査レポート | K |
| test taker | 被検査者 | K |
| tester | 検査者 | K |
| test-retest method | 再検査法, テスト・再テスト法 | K |
| texture gradient | 肌理(きめ)の勾配 | B |
| thanatos | タナトス, 死の欲動 | J |
| Thematic Apperception Test (TAT) | 絵画統覚検査, 主題統覚検査 | G J |
| theory of encounter group process | エンカウンターグループ過程理論 | J |
| theory of family relations | 家族関係論 | J |
| theory of mind | 心の理論 | |
| therapeutic alliance | 治療同盟 | J |
| therapeutic structure | 治療構造 | J |
| therapist | セラピスト, 治療者 | J |
| thinking | 思考 | D |
| threshold | 閾(いき)→ limen | B |
| Thurstone scale | サーストン尺度 | K |
| time limited psychotherapy | 時間制限心理療法 | J |
| time perception | 時間知覚 | B |
| title | (論文) タイトル, 表題, 題目 | K |
| token economy | トークン・エコノミー | C J |
| top-down processing | トップダウン処理 | D |
| topography | 局所論 | J |
| Tourette's disorder | トゥレット障害→ Gilles de la Tourette's syndrome | J |
| training group | Tグループ | J |
| trait theory | 特性論 | G |
| transactional analysis | 交流分析 | J |
| transactional model | 相乗的相互作用モデル | H |

| transference | 転移 | J |
| --- | --- | --- |
| transference psychosis | 転移精神病 | J |
| transitional object | 移行対象 | H J |
| transitional phase | 移行期, 過渡的な段階 | H J |
| transsexualism | 性転換（願望）症 | J |
| trauma | トラウマ, 外傷 | J |
| traumatic neurosis | 外傷神経症 | J |
| treatment | 治療 | J |
| tree drawing test | バウムテスト → Baumtest | G J |
| trickster | トリックスター | J |
| truancy | 怠学 | H J |
| true self | 真の自己, 本当の自己 | J |
| *t*-test | $t$ 検定 | K |
| twin study | 双生児研究 | K |
| two-store memory model | 記憶の二重貯蔵モデル | D |
| type I error | 第1種の過誤 | K |
| type II error | 第2種の過誤 | K |
| type theory | 類型論 | G |

## U

| unconditional positive regard | 無条件の肯定的関心 | J |
| --- | --- | --- |
| unconditioned stimulus | 無条件刺激 | C |
| unconscious | 無意識（の） | |
| under achiever | 学業不振児 | H |
| under-achievement | 学業不振 | H |
| undoing | 打ち消し | J |
| unidentified complaints | 不定愁訴 | J |
| utterance | 発話 | E |

## V

| | | |
|---|---|---|
| validity | 妥当性 | K |
| variable | 変数 | K |
| variance | 分散 | K |
| varimax rotation | バリマックス回転 | K |
| verbal | 言語的,言語性(の) | E G |
| verbal intelligence | 言語性知能 | G |
| vestibular sense | 平衡感覚 | B |
| vision | 視覚→ visual sense, sense of sight | B |
| visiting counseling | 訪問面接 | J |
| visual acuity | 視力 | B |
| visual illusion | 錯視 | B |
| visual sense | 視覚→ vision, sense of sight | B |
| visual-spatial orientation | 視空間的定位 | B |
| vocational aptitude test | 職業適性検査 | H I |
| volunteer activity | ボランティア活動 | I |
| voyeurism | 窃視症 | J |
| vulnerability | 脆弱性(ぜいじゃく) | H I J |

## W

| | | |
|---|---|---|
| WAIS | =Wechsler Adult Intelligence Scale | |
| Wechsler Adult Intelligence Scale (WAIS) | ウェクスラー成人知能検査 | G |
| Wechsler Intelligence Scale for Children (WISC) | ウェクスラー知能検査(児童・生徒用) | G |
| Wechsler Preschool and Primary Scale of Intelligence (WPPSI) | ウェクスラー知能検査(幼児用) | G |
| Wechsler-Bellevue Scale | ウェクスラー法 | G |
| we-consciousness | われわれ意識 | I |

| | | |
|---|---|---|
| we-consciousness feeling | = we-consciousness | |
| weighted average | 加重平均 | K |
| Wernicke's area | ウェルニッケ領域 | B E |
| WHO | = World Health Organization | |
| WISC | = Wechsler Intelligence Scale for Children | |
| wise old man | 老賢者 | J |
| wish | 願望 | D J |
| within-subject factor | 被験者内要因 | K |
| word association test | 言語連想実験 | J |
| workaholic | ワーカホリック，仕事中毒 | I J |
| working memory | 作業記憶，ワーキングメモリー | B C D |
| working through | 徹底操作 | J |
| workshop | ワークショップ | |
| World Health Organization（WHO） | 世界保健機関 | |
| WPPSI | =Wechsler Preschool and Primary Scale of Intelligence | |
| writer's cramp | 書痙 | J |

## Y

| | | |
|---|---|---|
| yes-tendency | イエス・テンデンシー，黙従傾向 | K |
| youth culture | ユース・カルチャー，若者文化 | I |

# 用語集
日本語→英語

## あ行

| | |
|---|---|
| IQ 得点 | IQ score |
| アイコンタクト | eye contact |
| アイゼンク性格検査 | Eysenck Personality Questionnaire (EPQ) → Maudsley Personality Inventory |
| 愛他主義 | ⇒利他主義 |
| 愛着 | ⇒アタッチメント |
| 愛着関係 | attachment relationship |
| アイデンティティ | identity |
| あいまい図形 | ⇒多義図形 |
| アウトサイダー | outsider |
| あがり | stage fright |
| 明るさ | lightness |
| アクション・リサーチ | action research |
| アクティブ・イマジネーション | active imagination |
| アクティブ・リスニング | active listening |
| アクティング・アウト | acting out |
| 悪夢 | nightmare → night terror／sleep terror |
| アサーション・トレーニング | assertion training |
| 欺き | deception |
| 足場（づくり） | scaffolding |
| 阿闍世コンプレックス | Ajase complex |

| | |
|---|---|
| アスペルガー症候群（障害） | Asperger syndrome／Asperger's disorder |
| アセスメント | assessment |
| 遊び | play |
| アタッチメント | attachment |
| アダプテーション | adaptation |
| アニマ | anima |
| アニミズム | animism |
| アニムス | animus |
| アノミー | anomy |
| アパシー | apathy |
| アブストラクト | abstract |
| アメリカ心理学会 | American Psychological Association（APA） |
| アメンチア | amentia |
| アルゴリズム | algorithm |
| アルコール依存症の | alcoholic |
| アルコール（依存）症 | alcoholism |
| アルツハイマー病 | Alzheimer's disease |
| アルファ係数 | coefficient alpha |
| アレキシサイミア | alexithymia |
| 暗示 | suggestion |
| 暗順応 | dark adaptation |
| 安全基地 | safety base／secure base |
| アンビバレンス | ambivalence |
| アンフェタミン | amphetamine → methamphetamine |
| 暗黙のパーソナリティ観 | implicit personaliry theory |
| イエス・テンデンシー | yes-tendency |
| 閾 | limen／threshold |
| 閾下知覚 | subliminal perception |
| 息どめ発作 | breath-holding spells |

## いげんせいしっかん

| | |
|---|---|
| 医原性疾患（医原病） | iatrogenic disease |
| 移行期 | transitional phase |
| 移行対象 | transitional object |
| 意識 | consciousness |
| 意識の | conscious |
| 意思決定 | decision making |
| いじめ | bullying |
| 異食 | pica |
| 依存 | dependence／dependency |
| 一元配置 | one-way layout |
| 一方向鏡 | ⇒マジック・ミラー |
| 一卵性双生児 | identical twins |
| 逸脱行動 | deviant behavior |
| 一致 | congruence |
| 一対比較法 | method of paired comparisons |
| 逸話的証拠 | anecdotal evidence |
| 偽り | ⇒欺き |
| 偽る | deceive |
| 遺伝 | heredity |
| 遺伝子 | gene |
| 遺伝子型 | genotype ⟷ phenotype |
| 遺伝の，遺伝に関する | genetic |
| 意図 | intention |
| イド | id = Es |
| イニシエーション | initiation |
| 異文化間カウンセリング | cross-cultural counseling |
| 異文化研究 | cross-cultural study |
| 今ここ | here and now |
| 意味記憶 | semantic memory |
| 意味ネットワーク | semantic network |

| | |
|---|---|
| 意味のある他者 | ⇒重要な他者 |
| 意味微分（法） | ⇒セマンティック・ディファレンシャル（法） |
| イメージ | image |
| 癒し | healing |
| イリノイ心理言語能力テスト | Illinois Test of Psycholinguistic Abilities（ITPA） |
| 色 | color |
| インクブロット | ink-blot |
| インクルージョン | inclusion |
| 因子 | factor |
| 因子分析 | factor analysis |
| 印象形成 | impression formation |
| 陰性転移 | negative transference ⟷ positive transference |
| インテーク面接 | intake interview |
| インフォーマル・グループ | informal group ⟷ formal group |
| インフォームド・コンセント | informed consent |
| インプリンティング | imprinting |
| 隠喩 | metaphor |
| 引用文献 | reference |
| ウェクスラー成人知能検査 | Wechsler Adult Intelligence Scale（WAIS） |
| ウェクスラー知能検査（児童・生徒用） | Wechsler Intelligence Scale for Children（WISC） |
| ウェクスラー知能検査（幼児用） | Wechsler Preschool and Primary Scale of Intelligence（WPPSI） |
| ウェクスラー法 | Wechsler-Bellevue Scale |
| ウェルニッケ領域 | Wernicke's area |
| 氏か育ちか | nature or nurture |
| 打ち消し | undoing |

## うつびょう

| | |
|---|---|
| うつ病 | depression／melancholia |
| 運動学 | kinesiology |
| 運動学習 | motor learning |
| 運動感覚 | kinesthesia |
| 運動技能 | motor skill |
| 運動制御 | motor control |
| 運動の知覚 | motion perception |
| 運動の不器用さ | motor clumsiness |
| エイジング | aging |
| エイズ | ⇒後天性免疫不全症候群 |
| HTPテスト | House-Tree-Person Test（HTP） |
| HTPPテスト | House-Tree-Person-Person Test（HTPP） |
| 栄養摂取 | nutrition |
| 疫学 | epidemiology |
| エゴグラム | egogram |
| エージェント | agent |
| エス | Es（独）＝id |
| SD（法） | ⇒セマンティック・ディファレンシャル（法） |
| エディプス期 | Oedipal phase |
| エディプス・コンプレックス | Oedipus complex |
| エピソード記憶 | episodic memory |
| $F$ 検定 | $F$ test |
| 演繹（法） | deduction ⟷ induction |
| エンカウンター | encounter |
| エンカウンター・グループ | encounter group |
| エンカウンターグループ過程理論 | theory of encounter group process |
| 遠刺激 | distal stimulus ⟷ proximal stimulus |
| 援助（する） | ⇒サポート |
| 援助行動 | helping behavior |

| | |
|---|---|
| 応諾 | ⇒コンプライアンス |
| 横断的研究 | cross-sectional study |
| 置き換え | displacement |
| 奥行き知覚 | depth perception |
| おとぎ話 | fairy tale |
| オピニオン・リーダー | opinion leader |
| オープンスクール | open school |
| オペラント条件づけ | operant conditioning |
| 親業訓練 | parent effectiveness training |
| 親子関係 | parent-child relationship |
| 音楽療法 | music therapy |
| 音源定位 | sound localization |
| 温情主義 | ⇒父性的干渉主義 |

## か 行

| | |
|---|---|
| 外因性の | exogenous ⟷ endogenous |
| 絵画統覚検査 | ⇒主題統覚検査 |
| 絵画療法 | art therapy |
| 回帰 | regression |
| 回帰分析 | regression analysis |
| 下位検査 | subtest |
| 外向性 | extraversion ⟷ introversion |
| 外在化 | externalization ⟷ internalization |
| 下意識 | subconsciousness |
| 下意識の | subconscious |
| カイ二乗（$\chi^2$）検定 | chi-square test |
| 解釈 | interpretation |
| 外傷 | ⇒トラウマ |
| 外傷後ストレス障害 | ⇒心的外傷後ストレス反応 |
| 外傷神経症 | traumatic neurosis |

## かいそうてききおく

| | |
|---|---|
| 回想的記憶 | retrospective memory |
| ガイダンス | guidance |
| 外的基準 | external criterion |
| 介入 | intervention |
| 概念 | concept |
| 概念駆動型処理 | conceptually driven processing |
| 概念形成 | concept formation |
| 海馬 | hippocampus |
| 外胚葉型 | ectomorphy |
| 開発 | development |
| 外発的動機づけ | extrinsic motivation ⟷ intrinsic motivation |
| 外罰的反応 | extrapunitive response |
| 回避―回避葛藤(かっとう) | avoidance-avoidance conflict |
| 回避学習 | avoidance learning |
| 快楽原則 | pleasure principle |
| 解離 | dissociation |
| 解離性同一性障害 | dissociative identity disorder |
| ガウス分布（正規分布） | Gauss distribution |
| カウンセリング | counseling |
| カウンターバランス | counterbalancing |
| 顔認識 | face recognition |
| 顔文字 | emoticon |
| 科学者―実践家モデル | scientist-practitioner model |
| 過換気症候群 | hyperventilation syndrome |
| 鍵刺激 | key stimulus |
| 画一性 | stereotype |
| 核家族 | nuclear family |
| 学業不振 | under-achievement |
| 学業不振児 | under achiever |
| 学習 | learning |

|  |  |
|---|---|
| 学習曲線 | learning curve |
| 学習障害 | learning disability（LD）／learning disorder（LD） |
| 学習する | learn |
| 学習性無力感 | learned helplessness |
| 学習の構え | learning set |
| 核心的同一性 | ⇒コア・アイデンティティ |
| 覚醒 | arousal |
| 学生相談 | student counseling |
| カクテルパーティ現象 | cocktail party phenomenon |
| カクテルパーティ効果 | cocktail party effect |
| 角膜 | cornea |
| 隔離 | isolation |
| 確率 | probability |
| 確率的判断 | probability judgment |
| 影 | shadow |
| 家系図 | ⇒ジェノグラム |
| 仮現運動 | apparent movement |
| 加重平均 | weighted average |
| 過剰適応 | over-adjustment |
| 過食 | binge eating → bulimia |
| 過食（症） | bulimia → binge eating |
| 仮性の | pseudo |
| 仮説 | assumption／hypothesis |
| 仮説検証 | hypothesis testing |
| 家族関係論 | theory of family relations |
| 可塑性 | plasticity |
| 硬さ | rigidity |
| 形の知覚 | form perception |
| かたより | ⇒バイアス |
| カタルシス | catharsis |

## がっこうこんさるてーしょん

| | |
|---|---|
| 学校コンサルテーション | school consultation |
| 学校心理士 | ⇒スクールサイコロジスト |
| 活性化拡散 | spreading activation |
| 葛藤(かっとう) | ⇒コンフリクト |
| 活動電位 | action potential |
| 過程尺度 | process scale |
| 家庭内暴力 | domestic violence (DV) |
| カテゴリー | category |
| カテゴリー化 | categorization |
| 過渡的な段階 | ⇒移行期 |
| 過眠(症) | hypersomnia |
| カルチャーショック | culture shock |
| カルト | cult |
| 寛解 | remission |
| 感覚 | sensation / sense |
| 間隔尺度 | interval scale |
| 感覚モダリティ | sense modality → modality |
| 喚起 | arousal |
| 眼球運動 | eye movement |
| 眼球輻輳(ふくそう)運動 | ⇒輻輳運動 |
| 環境 | environment |
| 環境療法 | milieu therapy |
| 間欠強化 | intermittent reinforcement |
| 観察 | observation |
| 観察学習 | observational learning |
| 観察する | observe |
| 患者とみなされた者 | identified patient (IP) |
| 慣習 | custom |
| 間(かん)主観性 | intersubjectivity |
| 感受性訓練 | sensitivity training |

| | |
|---|---|
| 感情 | affect ／ affection |
| 感情混入モデル | Affect-Infusion Model |
| 感情情報機能説 | feeling-as-information |
| 感情表出 | emotional expression |
| 関心 | interest |
| 感応 | induction |
| 願望 | wish |
| 緘黙（症） | mutism |
| 関与 | ⇒コミットメント |
| 関与しながらの観察 | participant observation |
| 記憶 | memory |
| 記憶の二重貯蔵モデル | two-store memory model |
| 記憶範囲 | memory span |
| 記憶容量 | memory span |
| 幾何学的錯視 | geometrical illusion |
| 利き足 | footedness |
| 危機介入 | crisis intervention |
| 利き手 | handedness |
| 記号 | sign |
| 記号化 | ⇒符号化 |
| 気質 | temperament |
| 器質精神病 | organic psychosis |
| 擬似の | pseudo |
| 記述 | description |
| 記述統計学 | descriptive statistics |
| 基準関連妥当性 | criterion-related validity |
| 帰属 | attribution |
| 議題設定 | agenda-setting |
| 期待値 | expected value |
| 吃音 | stuttering |

# きづき

| | |
|---|---|
| 気づき | awareness |
| 輝度 | luminance |
| 帰納（法） | induction ⟷ deduction |
| 技能 | skill |
| 機能局在論 | localization theory |
| 機能主義 | functionalism |
| 機能障害 | functional disorder ／ impairment |
| 機能する | operate |
| 帰納的思考 | inductive thinking |
| 機能的自律性 | functional autonomy |
| キーパーソン | key-person |
| 気晴らし | distraction |
| 気晴らし食い | binge eating → bulimia |
| 気分 | mood |
| 気分依存記憶 | mood-dependent memory |
| 気分一致記憶 | mood-congruent memory |
| 基本的信頼 | basic trust |
| 帰無仮説 | null hypothesis |
| 記銘 | memorization |
| 肌理(きめ)の勾配 | texture gradient |
| 偽薬 | placebo |
| 虐待 | abuse |
| 脚本分析 | script analysis |
| 客観的な | objective ⟷ subjective |
| 逆向条件づけ | backward conditioning |
| 逆向抑制 | retroactive inhibition ⟷ proactive inhibition |
| キャリア開発 | career development |
| キャリア・カウンセリング | career counseling |
| キャリア発達 | career development |
| キャリーオーバー効果 | carry-over effect |

| | |
|---|---|
| ギャングエイジ | gang age |
| ギャンブラーの誤謬 | gambler's fallacy |
| 嗅覚 | olfaction / olfactory sense / sense of smell |
| 急性精神病 | acute psychosis |
| 急速眼球運動 | ⇒レム |
| 教育相談 | educational counseling |
| 鏡映的自己 | looking-glass self |
| 鏡映描写 | mirror drawing |
| 強化 | reinforcement |
| 境界人 | marginal man |
| 境界性パーソナリティ障害 | borderline personality disorder |
| 境界例 | borderline case |
| 共感 | empathy |
| 共感覚 | synesthesia |
| 競合 | competition |
| 教示 | instruction |
| 凝視 | fixation |
| 教師カウンセラー | teacher counselor |
| 教示する | instruct |
| 共時性 | synchronicity |
| 教授 | instruction |
| 凝集性 | cohesiveness |
| 共生 | symbiosis |
| 強制選択 | forced choice |
| 強制的 | compulsive → obsessive |
| 競争 | competition |
| きょうだい関係 | siblings relationship |
| 協調運動障害 | incoordination |
| 共通性 | communality |
| 共同注意 | ⇒ジョイント・アテンション |

きょうどうちゅうし

| | |
|---|---|
| 共同注視 | ⇒ジョイント・アテンション |
| 強迫観念 | obsession |
| 強迫行為 | compulsion |
| 強迫神経症 | obsessional neurosis |
| 強迫性障害（強迫症） | obsessive-compulsive disorder（OCD） |
| 強迫性の | ⇒強迫的 |
| 強迫的 | compulsive／obsessive |
| 恐怖 | fear |
| 恐怖喚起コミュニケーション | fear-arousing communication |
| 恐怖管理理論 | terror-management theory |
| 恐怖症 | phobia |
| 共分散 | covariance |
| 共分散構造分析 | covariance structure analysis |
| 共分散分析 | analysis of covariance |
| 興味 | interest |
| （研究・調査への）協力者 | ⇒参加者 |
| 虚偽尺度 | lie scale |
| 極限法 | method of limits |
| 局在（化） | localization |
| 局所論 | topography |
| 巨視的行動 | macroscopic behavior ⟵⟶ microscopic behavior → molar behavior |
| 去勢不安 | castration anxiety |
| 拒絶症 | negativism |
| 拒否症 | ⇒拒絶症 |
| 筋緊張 | muscle tone |
| 筋緊張亢進 | hypertonia |
| 禁止 | inhibition → suppression |
| 近刺激 | proximal stimulus ⟵⟶ distal stimulus |

| | |
|---|---|
| 近親姦 | incest |
| 筋電図 | electromyography (EMG) |
| 筋力 | muscle strength |
| 空間知覚 | space perception |
| 空想 | fantasy／phantasy |
| 偶発学習 | incidental learning |
| グッドイナフ・テスト | Goodenough Draw-a-Man test → Draw-a-Man test |
| クライエント | client |
| クラスター | cluster |
| クラスター分析 | cluster analysis |
| グラフ理論 | graph theory |
| グループ・スーパービジョン | group supervision |
| グループ・ダイナミクス | group dynamics |
| クロス集計表 | cross table |
| 群 | cluster／group |
| 群集 | crowd |
| (研究，要因) 計画 | design → experimental design |
| 経験 | experience |
| 経験主義 | empiricism |
| 経験論 | ⇒経験主義 |
| 迎合 | ingratiation |
| 計算論的アプローチ | computational approach |
| 芸術療法 | art therapy |
| 傾聴 | ⇒アクティブ・リスニング |
| 頚定（けいてい） | head control |
| 系統発生 | phylogeny ⟵⟶ ontogeny |
| 傾眠 | drowsiness |
| 係留効果 | anchoring effect |
| 系列位置効果 | serial position effect |
| ゲシュタルト | Gestalt (独) |

| | |
|---|---|
| ケース・カンファレンス | case conference |
| ケース・スタディ | case study |
| ゲス・フー・テスト | guess-who test |
| 結果 | result |
| 月経前症候群 | premenstrual syndrome |
| 結婚カウンセリング | marriage counseling |
| 結晶性知能 | crystallized intelligence |
| 欠損値 | missing value |
| ゲーム分析 | game analysis |
| 権威主義的パーソナリティ | authoritarian personality |
| 原因帰属 | causal attribution |
| 幻覚 | hallucination |
| 限局的興味 | limited interest |
| 元型 | archetype |
| 言語 | language |
| 原光景 | primal scene |
| 健康心理学 | health psychology |
| 言語獲得 | language acquisition |
| 言語性知能 | verbal intelligence |
| 言語性の | verbal |
| 言語的 | ⇒言語性（の） |
| 言語療法士 | ⇒スピーチ・セラピスト |
| 言語連想実験 | word association test |
| 検査（テスト） | test |
| 顕在記憶 | explicit memory |
| 検索 | retrieval |
| 検索手がかり | retrieval cue |
| 検査者 | tester |
| 検査レポート | test report |
| 幻肢 | phantom limb |

| | |
|---|---|
| 現実感喪失 | derealization |
| 現実吟味 | reality testing |
| 現実原則 | reality principle |
| 現実検討 | ⇒現実吟味 |
| 原始的防衛機制 | primitive defense mechanism |
| 原始的理想化 | primitive idealization |
| 検出力 | ⇒統計検定力 |
| 現象学 | phenomenology |
| 現象学的心理学 | phenomenological psychology |
| 幻想 | phantasy → fantasy |
| 現存在分析(実存分析) | existential analysis |
| 検定 | test |
| 検定力 | ⇒統計検定力 |
| 見当識 | orientation |
| 現場実験 | ⇒フィールド実験 |
| 健忘(症) | amnesia |
| コア・アイデンティティ | core identity |
| 行為化 | ⇒アクティング・アウト |
| 行為障害 | conduct disorder |
| 構音障害 | dysarthria |
| 効果 | effect |
| 効果器 | effector |
| 交感神経系 | sympathetic nervous system (SNS) |
| 好奇心 | curiosity |
| 高機能自閉症 | high-functioning autism |
| 攻撃性 | aggression |
| 高原現象 | ⇒プラトー現象 |
| 交互作用 | interaction |
| 交互作用効果 | interaction effect |
| (論文)考察 | discussion |

| | |
|---|---|
| 公式集団 | ⇒フォーマル・グループ |
| 高次脳機能 | higher brain function |
| 恒常刺激法 | method of constant stimuli<br>→ constant method |
| 恒常状態 | ⇒ホメオスタシス |
| 恒常性 | constancy |
| 恒常法 | constant method<br>／method of constant stimuli |
| 口唇期（こうしんき） | oral phase |
| 構成概念妥当性 | construct validity |
| 後成説 | epigenesis |
| 肯定的感情 | positive emotion<br>⟵⟶ negative emotion |
| 肯定的幻想 | ⇒ポジティブ・イリュージョン |
| 後天性免疫不全症候群 | Acquired Immunodeficiency Syndrome（AIDS） |
| 行動 | behavior |
| 行動化 | ⇒アクティング・アウト |
| 行動カウンセリング | behavioral counseling |
| 合同家族療法 | conjoint family therapy |
| 行動観察 | behavior observation |
| 行動主義 | behaviorism |
| 行動主義アプローチ | behaviorist approach |
| 行動生物学 | ⇒比較行動学 |
| 合同面接 | conjoint counseling |
| 行動療法 | behavior therapy |
| 校内暴力 | school violence |
| 広汎性発達障害（こうはん） | pervasive developmental disorder（PDD） |
| 興奮転移理論 | excitation transfer theory |
| 公平 | equity |
| 衡平（こうへい） | equity |

| | |
|---|---|
| 項目反応理論 | item response theory |
| 項目分析 | item analysis |
| 肛門期 | anal phase |
| 合理化 | rationalization |
| 効率 | efficiency |
| 交流分析 | transactional analysis |
| 国際疾病分類 | International Classification of Diseases (ICD) |
| 国民性 | national character |
| 互恵的利他主義 | reciprocal altruism |
| 心の理論 | theory of mind |
| 固執(こしゅう) | perseveration |
| 誤診 | misdiagnosis |
| 個人間の | interindividual ⟷ intraindividual / interpersonal ⟷ intrapersonal |
| 個人空間 | ⇒パーソナル・スペース |
| 個人差 | individual differences |
| 個人的無意識 | individual unconscious |
| 個人内の | intraindividual ⟷ interindividual / intrapersonal ⟷ interpersonal |
| 個性化過程 | individuation process |
| 個性記述的研究 | idiographic method |
| 個体発生 | ontogeny ⟷ phylogeny |
| 固着 | fixation |
| ごっこ遊び | pretend play |
| 固定的運動型 | ⇒固定的動作パターン |
| 固定的活動型 | ⇒固定的動作パターン |
| 固定的動作パターン | fixed action pattern (FAP) |
| 古典的条件づけ | classical conditioning |
| コード化する | code |
| コネクショニズム | connectionism |

## こーぴんぐ

| | |
|---|---|
| コーピング | coping |
| コホート | cohort |
| コミットメント | commitment |
| コミュニティ | community |
| コミュニティ心理学 | community psychology |
| 固有値 | eigenvalue |
| 語用機能 | pragmatic function |
| 語用機能障害 | pragmatic dysfunction |
| コラージュ療法 | collage therapy |
| 孤立 | isolation |
| コンサルテーション | consultation |
| コンピテンス | competence |
| コンピュータ援用学習システム | computer assisted instruction (CAI) |
| コンピュータを介したコミュニケーション | computer-mediated communication (CMC) |
| コンプライアンス | compliance |
| コンフリクト | conflict |
| コンプレックス | complex |
| 昏迷 | stupor |

## さ 行

| | |
|---|---|
| 再検査法 | test-retest method |
| サイコセラピスト | psychotherapist |
| 最小有意差 | least significant difference (*LSD*) |
| 再生 | recall |
| 最適化 | optimization |
| 採点 | ⇒スコアリング |
| 再認 | recognition |
| 最頻値 | ⇒モード |
| 催眠 | hypnosis |

| | |
|---|---|
| 催眠療法 | hypnotherapy |
| 最尤推定法 | maximum likelihood estimate method ／ maximum likelihood estimation method |
| サイン検定 | sign test |
| 作業記憶 | ⇒ワーキングメモリー |
| 作業検査 | performance test |
| 作業療法 | occupational therapy（OT） |
| 錯視 | visual illusion |
| サクラ | ⇒実験共謀協力者 |
| 錯乱 | confusion |
| サーストン尺度 | Thurstone scale |
| 錯覚 | illusion |
| 査定 | ⇒アセスメント |
| サディズム | sadism ⟷ masochism |
| 悟り | enlightenment |
| サブカルチャー | subculture |
| 差別 | discrimination |
| サポート | support |
| （研究・調査への）参加者 | participant → subject |
| 産業カウンセリング | industrial counseling |
| 残効 | after effect |
| 残差 | residual |
| 参照枠 | frame of reference |
| 残像 | after image |
| サンプリング | sampling |
| サンプル | sample |
| 参与観察 | participant observation |
| ジェスチャー | gesture |
| ジェノグラム | genogram |
| シェマ | schema |

じぇんだー

| | |
|---|---|
| ジェンダー | gender |
| 自我 | ego |
| 自我関与 | ego-involvement |
| 自我機能 | ego function |
| 視覚 | vision ／ visual sense ／ sense of sight |
| 自覚 | self-awareness |
| 自家中毒 | auto-intoxication |
| 自我同一性 | ego-identity |
| 自我の強さ | ego-strength ⟷ ego-weakness |
| 自我の弱さ | ego-weakness ⟷ ego-strength |
| 時間制限心理療法 | time limited psychotherapy |
| 時間知覚 | time perception |
| 士気 | ⇒モラール |
| 磁気共鳴画像 | magnetic resonance imaging (MRI) |
| 色聴 | colored hearing |
| 色盲 | color blindness |
| 視空間的定位 | visual-spatial orientation |
| 軸索突起 | axon |
| 刺激 | stimulation ／ stimulus |
| 資源 | resource |
| 自己 | self |
| 自己愛 | ⇒ナルシシズム |
| 自己愛人格障害 | narcissistic personality disorder |
| 自己意識 | self-consciousness |
| 志向 | intention |
| 思考 | thinking |
| 思考散乱 | ⇒支離滅裂 |
| 自己概念 | self-concept |
| 自己覚知 | self-awareness |

| | |
|---|---|
| 自己高揚 | self-enhancement |
| 自己効力感 | ⇒セルフ・エフィカシー |
| 自己実現 | self-actualization |
| 自己主張訓練 | ⇒アサーション・トレーニング |
| 自己受容 | self-acceptance |
| 事後情報効果 | post-event information effect |
| 自己心理学 | self psychology |
| 自己中心語 | egocentric speech |
| 自己中心性 | egocentrism |
| 自己呈示(提示) | self-presentation |
| 自己統制法 | self control |
| 仕事中毒 | ⇒ワーカホリック |
| 事後の | post hoc ⟷ prior |
| 自己評価 | self-evaluation |
| 自己分析 | self-analysis |
| 自殺 | suicide |
| 支持 | support |
| 指示的カウンセリング | directive counseling |
| 思春期 | puberty |
| 思春期内閉症 | juvenile seclusion |
| 自傷 | self-mutilation |
| 視床下部 | hypothalamus |
| 事象関連電位 | event-related potential (ERP) |
| 自助グループ | ⇒セルフヘルプ・グループ |
| 自叙伝法 | autobiographical method |
| 視神経 | optic nerve |
| 視神経交叉 | optic chiasm |
| システムズ・アプローチ | systems approach |
| 姿勢(時)振戦 | postural tremor |
| 施設病 | ⇒ホスピタリズム |

| | |
|---|---|
| 視線回避 | gaze aversion |
| 自然観察 | naturalistic observation |
| 自然言語処理 | natural language processing |
| 自然選択 | ⇒自然淘汰 |
| 自然治癒力 | spontaneous remission |
| 自然淘汰 | natural selection |
| 事前の | prior ⟷ post hoc |
| 視線の交錯 | ⇒アイコンタクト |
| 自尊感情 | ⇒自尊心 |
| 自尊心 | self-esteem |
| 失感情表現症 | ⇒アレキシサイミア |
| 実験 | experiment |
| 実験共謀協力者 | confederate ⟷ naive participant |
| 実験群 | experimental group |
| 実験計画法 | experimental design |
| 実験室 | laboratory |
| 実験者 | experimenter |
| 実験者効果 | experimenter effect |
| 実験条件 | experimental condition |
| 失語（症） | aphasia |
| 失行（症） | apraxia |
| 実証に基づく心理療法 | evidence-based psychotherapy |
| 失神 | syncope |
| 嫉妬 | jealousy |
| 失読症 | alexia |
| 失認（症） | agnosia |
| 疾病利得 | gain from illness |
| 質問紙 | questionnaire |
| 私的発話 | private speech |
| 指導 | ⇒ガイダンス |
| 自動運動 | autokinetic movement |

| | |
|---|---|
| 児童絵画統覚検査 | Children's Apperception Test (CAT) |
| 児童期 | middle childhood |
| 自動的過程 | automatic process |
| シナプス | synapse |
| 死の欲動 | ⇒タナトス |
| 示範 | exemplification |
| G-P分析 | good-poor analysis (G-P analysis) |
| 指標となる患者 | identified patient (IP) |
| 自閉(症) | autism |
| 自閉症スペクトラム障害 | autistic spectrum disorders |
| 嗜癖 | addiction |
| シミュレーション | simulation |
| 社会化 | socialization |
| 社会構築主義 | social constructivism |
| 社会性 | sociability |
| 社会調査 | social survey |
| 社会的アイデンティティ理論 | social identity theory |
| 社会的学習理論 | social learning theory |
| 社会的価値 | social value |
| 社会的規範 | social norm |
| 社会的コンピテンス | social competence |
| 社会的参照 | ⇒ソーシャル・リファレンス |
| 社会的スキル | ⇒ソーシャル・スキル |
| 社会的性格 | social character |
| 社会的文脈 | social context |
| 社会病質 | sociopathy |
| 社会復帰 | ⇒リハビリテーション |
| 尺度 | scale |
| 尺度構成法 | scaling method |
| 遮断効果 | masking effect |

| | |
|---|---|
| シャーマン | shaman |
| 重回帰分析 | multiple regression analysis |
| 習慣 | habit |
| 習慣強度 | habit strength |
| 集合行動 | collective behavior |
| 集合的無意識 | collective unconscious |
| 自由再生 | free recall |
| 周産期 | perinatal period |
| 重相関 | multiple correlation |
| 重相関係数 | multiple correlation coefficient |
| 収束的妥当性 | convergent validity |
| 従属変数 | dependent variable |
| 集団規範 | group norm |
| 集団成極化 | group polarization |
| 縦断的研究 | longitudinal study |
| 集団力学 | ⇒グループ・ダイナミクス |
| 自由度 | degree of freedom ($df$) |
| 重度心身障害 | severe mental and physical disability |
| 習癖性障害 | habit disorder |
| 周辺人 | ⇒境界人 |
| 重要な他者 | significant others |
| 自由連想 | free association |
| 主観的な | subjective ⟷ objective |
| 主効果 | main effect |
| 主成分分析 | principal component analysis |
| 主題統覚検査 | Thematic Apperception Test (TAT) |
| 出現頻度 | frequency of occurrence |
| 出産外傷 | birth trauma |
| 出生前期 | prenatal period |
| 守秘 | ⇒秘密保持 |
| 受容 | acceptance |

| | |
|---|---|
| 受容器 | receptor cell |
| 受容野 | receptive field |
| 受理面接 | ⇒インテーク面接 |
| 順位相関係数 | rank order correlation coefficient |
| 順位法 | method of rank order |
| 馴化 | ⇒慣れ |
| 循環気質 | cyclothymia |
| 準拠集団 | ⇒リファレンス・グループ |
| 準拠枠 | ⇒参照枠 |
| 順向抑制 | proactive inhibition<br>⟷ retroactive inhibition |
| 準実験計画 | quasi-experimental design |
| 順序尺度 | ordinal scale |
| 順応 | ⇒アダプテーション |
| ジョイント・アテンション | joint attention |
| 上位―下位分析 | ⇒ G-P 分析 |
| 昇華 | sublimation |
| 浄化 | ⇒カタルシス |
| (能力の) 障害 | disability |
| 障害児 | disabled child |
| 生涯発達 | life-span development |
| 小奇形 | minor anomaly |
| 消去 | extinction |
| (独立変数の要因における) 条件 | condition |
| 条件づけ | conditioning |
| 条件反射 | conditioned reflex |
| 症候移動 | syndrome shift |
| 症候群 | ⇒シンドローム |
| 小視症 | micropsia |
| 小字症 | micrographia |
| 成就指数 | accomplishment quotient (AQ) |

## しょうじょう

| | |
|---|---|
| 症状 | symptom |
| 症状形成 | symptom formation |
| 少数者 | ⇒マイノリティ |
| 承諾 | ⇒コンプライアンス |
| 承諾先取り法 | low-ball technique |
| 象徴 | symbol |
| 象徴機能 | symbolic function |
| 情緒障害 | emotional disturbance |
| 情緒剥奪(はくだつ) | emotional deprivation |
| 衝動 | impulse |
| 情動 | emotion |
| 常同行為 | stereotypic action |
| 衝動行動 | impulsive behavior |
| 常同症 | stereotypy |
| 情動制御 | emotion regulation |
| 情動知能 | emotional intelligence |
| 常同的行動 | stereotypic behavior |
| 少年非行 | juvenile delinquency |
| 小脳 | cerebellum |
| 情報処理 | information processing |
| 情報的影響 | informational influence |
| 譲歩的要請法 | door-in-the-face technique |
| 剰余変数 | extraneous variable |
| 初回面接 | ⇒インテーク面接 |
| 職業適性検査 | vocational aptitude test |
| 書痙(しょけい) | writer's cramp |
| 触覚 | tactile sense ／ sense of touch |
| 初頭効果 | primacy effect |
| 初頭努力 | initial spurt |
| 処理資源 | processing resource |
| 自立 | independence |

|  |  |
|---|---|
| 自律訓練法 | autogenic training |
| 自律神経系 | autonomic nervous system (ANS) |
| 自律神経失調症 | autonomic dystonia |
| 支離滅裂 | incoherence |
| 視力 | visual acuity |
| ジル・ド・ラ・トゥレット症候群 | Gilles de la Tourette's syndrome → Tourette's disorder |
| 事例研究 | ⇒ケース・スタディ |
| 事例検討会 | ⇒ケース・カンファレンス |
| 心因性反応 | psychogenic reaction |
| 心因の | psychogenic |
| 人格 | ⇒パーソナリティ |
| 人格検査 | personality test |
| 人格障害 | personality disorder |
| 心気症 | hypochondriasis |
| 親近効果 | ⇒新近効果 |
| 新近効果 | recency effect |
| シングル・ペアレント | single parent |
| 神経系 | nervous system |
| 神経症 | neurosis |
| 神経心理学 | neuropsychology |
| 神経性食欲不振症 | anorexia nervosa |
| 神経節 | ganglion |
| 神経伝達物質 | neurotransmitter |
| 信号検出理論 | signal detection theory |
| 人工知能 | artificial intelligence |
| 人口統計学的特性 | demographic trait |
| 新行動主義 | neo-behaviorism |
| 心身症 | psychosomatic disease |
| 心身相関 | mind-body correlation |
| 新生児 | neonate ／ newborn child |

| | |
|---|---|
| 深層心理学 | depth psychology |
| 身体イメージ | body image |
| 身体化障害 | somatization disorder |
| 身体言語 | ⇒ボディ・ランゲージ |
| 身体図式 | body schema |
| 身体像 | ⇒身体イメージ |
| 身体的な | physical |
| 身体認知障害 | somatognostic disorder |
| 診断 | diagnosis |
| 診断（的）検査 | diagnostic test |
| 診断する | diagnose |
| 心的イメージ | mental imagery |
| 心的エネルギー | psychic energy |
| 心的外傷 | psychic trauma |
| 心的外傷後ストレス障害 | post-traumatic stress disorder (PTSD) |
| 心的回転 | mental rotation |
| 人的資源管理 | human resources management |
| 心的努力 | mental effort |
| 心的飽和 | mental saturation |
| 心電図 | electrocardiogram |
| シンドローム | syndrome |
| 侵入 | ⇒インクルージョン |
| 信念 | belief |
| 真の自己 | true self |
| 信憑性（しんぴょうせい） | credibility |
| 人物画知能検査 | Draw-a-Man test (DAM) ／ Goodenough Draw-a-Man test |
| 人物画テスト | Draw-a-Person test (DAP) |
| 親密化過程 | close relationship process |
| 親密さ | intimacy |

| | |
|---|---|
| 信頼性 | reliability |
| 心理アセスメント | psychological assessment |
| 心理学者 | psychologist |
| 心理教育 | psychoeducation |
| 心理言語学 | psycholinguistics |
| 心理査定 | ⇒心理アセスメント |
| 心理社会的性 | ⇒ジェンダー |
| 心理社会的危機 | psycho-social crisis |
| 心理診断 | ⇒心理アセスメント |
| 心理テスト | psychological test |
| 心理物理学 | ⇒精神物理学 |
| 心理療法 | psychotherapy |
| 心理療法士 | ⇒サイコセラピスト |
| 人類 | human beings |
| 神話 | myth |
| 親和動機 | affiliation motive |
| 水準 | level |
| 錐体(すいたい) | cone |
| 随伴陰性変動 | contingent negative variation (CNV) |
| 随伴性 | contingency |
| 睡眠障害 | sleep disorder |
| 水路づけ | canalization |
| 推論 | inference / reasonng |
| スキーマ | schema |
| スクリーニング | screening |
| スクリーニング・テスト | screening test |
| スクールカウンセラー | school counselor |
| スクールサイコロジスト | school psychologist |
| スクール・ソーシャルワーク | school social work |
| 図形残効 | figural after-effect |

## すけーぷごーと

| | |
|---|---|
| スケープゴート（説） | scapegoat |
| スコアリング | scoring |
| スタンフォード・ビネー知能検査 | Stanford-Binet Intelligence test |
| スティーヴンスの法則 | Stevens' law |
| ステップワイズ変数選択 | step-wise selection |
| ステレオタイプ | stereotype |
| 図と地 | figure and ground |
| ストループテスト | stroop test |
| ストレス | stress |
| ストレッサー | stressor |
| ストレンジ・シチュエーション法 | strange situation procedure |
| ストローク | stroke |
| スーパーバイザー | supervisor |
| スーパーバイジー | supervisee |
| スーパービジョン | supervision |
| スピーチ・セラピスト | speech therapist（ST） |
| 刷り込み | ⇒インプリンティング |
| 生育史 | ⇒生活史 |
| 性格 | character |
| 性格検査 | ⇒人格検査 |
| 生活史 | life history |
| 生活年齢 | chronological age（CA） |
| 生活の質 | quality of life（QOL） |
| 生活歴 | ⇒生活史 |
| 性器期 | genital phase |
| 正規分布 | normal distribution |
| 制御的過程 | controlled process |
| 制限 | restriction |
| 制止 | inhibition → suppression |
| 制止する | inhibit → suppress |
| 脆弱性（ぜいじゃく） | vulnerability |

| | |
|---|---|
| 成熟 | maturation |
| 正準相関分析 | canonical correlation analysis |
| 精神衛生 | mental health |
| 精神科医 | psychiatrist |
| 精神障害 | mental disorder |
| 精神障害の診断・統計マニュアル | Diagnostic and Statistical Manual of Mental Disorders (DSM) |
| 精神遅滞 | mental retardation |
| 精神年齢 | mental age (MA) |
| 精神病 | psychosis |
| 精神病質 | psychopathy |
| 精神病理(学) | psychopathology |
| 精神物理学 | psychophysics |
| 精神物理学的測定法 | psychophysical methods |
| 精神分析 | psychoanalysis |
| 精神力動(論) | psychodynamics |
| 精神療法 | ⇒心理療法 |
| 生成文法 | generative grammar |
| 精緻化 | elaboration |
| 成長 | growth |
| 成長モデル | growth model |
| 性的外傷 | sexual trauma |
| 性的虐待 | sexual abuse |
| 性的倒錯 | sexual perversion |
| 性的二型 | sexual dimorphism |
| 性的ハラスメント | sexual harassment |
| 性転換(願望)症 | transsexualism |
| 性同一性障害 | gender identity disorder |
| 生得的行動 | innate behavior |
| 生得的性質 | nature |
| 生得論 | nativism |

## せいどけんさ

| | |
|---|---|
| 性度検査 | masculinity-femininity scale |
| 生徒指導 | student guidance |
| 青年期 | adolescence |
| 正の | positive ⟷ negative |
| 制約 | constraint |
| 性役割 | sex role |
| 性欲動論 | sexual drive theory |
| 生理的反応 | biological response |
| 世界保健機関 | World Health Organization (WHO) |
| 世代間境界 | generation boundary |
| 接近―回避葛藤 | approach-avoidance conflict |
| 接近―接近葛藤 | approach-approach conflict |
| セックス・カウンセリング | sex counseling |
| 窃視症 | voyeurism |
| 接種理論 | inoculation theory |
| 摂食障害 | eating disorder |
| 摂食中枢 | feeding center |
| 絶対閾 | absolute threshold |
| 折衷主義 | eclecticism |
| 説明による同意 | ⇒インフォームド・コンセント |
| セマンティック・ディファレンシャル | semantic differential (SD) |
| セマンティック・ディファレンシャル法 | semantic differential method |
| セラピスト | therapist |
| セルフ・エフィカシー | self-efficacy |
| セルフ・ハンディキャッピング | self-handicapping |
| セルフヘルプ・グループ | self help group |
| セルフ・モニタリング | self-monitoring |
| セロトニン | serotonin |
| 前意識（の） | preconscious |
| 宣言的記憶 | declarative memory |

| | |
|---|---|
| 宣言的知識 | declarative knowledge |
| 先行研究 | preceding study |
| 潜在学習 | latent learning |
| 潜在記憶 | implicit memory |
| 潜時 | latency |
| 染色体 | chromosome |
| 染色体異常 | chromosomal aberration |
| 漸成説 | ⇒後成説 |
| 全体論 | holism |
| 選択的注意 | selective attention |
| 先天性精神遅滞 | ⇒アメンチア |
| 前頭前野 | prefrontal cortex |
| 前頭葉 | frontal lobe |
| 前頭連合野 | frontal association area |
| 洗脳 | brainwashing |
| 潜伏期 | latency period |
| 羨望(せんぼう) | envy |
| 前方視的研究 | prospective study |
| せん妄 | delirium |
| 戦略 | strategy |
| 相関 | correlation |
| 相関係数 | correlation coefficient |
| 早期幼児自閉症 | early infantile autism |
| 相互依存性 | interdependency |
| 相互協調的自己感 | interdependent self |
| 相互作用 | interaction |
| 相互独立的自己観 | independent self |
| 操作主義 | operationalism / operationism |
| 操作的定義 | operational definition |
| 相似 | analogy ⟷ homology |

| | |
|---|---|
| 相乗的相互作用モデル | transactional model |
| 走性 | taxis |
| 双生児研究 | twin study |
| 想像 | imagination |
| 創造性 | creativity |
| 総体的行動 | ⇒モル的行動 |
| 相対的な | relative |
| 相対評価 | relative evaluation |
| 躁的防衛 | manic defense |
| 相同 | homology ⟷ analogy |
| 促進 | ⇒ファシリテーション |
| 側性化 | lateralization |
| 測定 | measurement |
| 測度 | measure |
| 側頭葉 | temporal lobe |
| ソシオグラム | sociogram |
| ソシオドラマ | sociodrama |
| ソシオマトリックス | sociomatrix |
| ソシオメトリー | sociometry |
| ソシオメトリック・テスト | Sociometric Test |
| 素質 | disposition |
| ソーシャル・サポート | social support |
| ソーシャル・スキル | social skill |
| ソーシャル・スキルトレーニング | social skill training (SST) |
| ソーシャルワーク | social work |
| ソーシャル・リファレンス | social reference |
| ソース・モニタリング | source monitoring |
| その場限りの,その場しのぎの | ad hoc |
| 素朴理論 | naive theory |
| ソンディ・テスト | Szondi Test |

## た 行

| | |
|---|---|
| 第1種の過誤 | type I error |
| 体液 | humor |
| 怠学 | truancy |
| 対決 | confrontation |
| 体験過程 | experiencing |
| 退行 | regression |
| 胎児期 | fetal period |
| 体質 | constitution |
| 対処 | ⇒コーピング |
| 対照群 | ⇒統制群 |
| 対象恒常性 | object constancy |
| 対象喪失 | object loss |
| 対人関係 | interpersonal relations |
| 対人関係論 | interpersonal theory |
| 対人恐怖 | anthropophobia |
| 対人的な | interpersonal ⟷ intrapersonal |
| 対人認知 | interpersonal cognition |
| 対人魅力 | interpersonal attraction |
| 態勢 | ⇒ポジション |
| 体制化 | organization |
| 体性感覚 | somatic sense |
| 態度 | attitude |
| (論文) タイトル | title |
| 第二言語 | second language |
| 第二次性徴 | secondary sex characteristics |
| 第2種の過誤 | type II error |
| 大脳 | cerebrum |
| 大脳皮質 | cerebral cortex |
| 大脳辺縁系 | limbic system |

たいはい

| | |
|---|---|
| 胎胚(たいはい) | embryo |
| 対比 | contrast |
| 代表値 | average |
| （論文）題目 | ⇒タイトル |
| 対立仮説 | alternative hypothesis |
| ダウン症候群 | Down's syndrome |
| 多義図形 | ambiguous figure |
| 多次元尺度構成法 | multidimensional scaling（MDS） |
| 多肢選択 | multiple choice |
| 他視点取得 | perspective-taking |
| 多重共線性 | multicollinearity |
| 多重人格 | multiple personality |
| 多重比較 | multiple comparison |
| 多数者 | ⇒マジョリティ |
| 脱感作 | desensitization |
| 抱っこ | holding |
| 脱個人化 | depersonalization |
| 達成動機 | achievement motive |
| 妥当性 | validity |
| タナトス | thanatos |
| ダブルバインド | double bind |
| ダブルバーレル質問 | double-barreled question |
| 多変量解析 | multivariate analysis |
| 多変量分散分析 | multivariate analysis of variance（MANOVA） |
| ダミー変数 | dummy variable |
| 段階的要請法 | foot-in-the-door technique |
| 短期記憶 | short-term memory |
| 男根期 | phallic phase |
| 探索行動 | exploratory behavior |
| 単純主効果 | simple main effect |

| | |
|---|---|
| 単親 | ⇒シングル・ペアレント |
| 弾力性 | resilience |
| 談話 | discourse |
| 地域社会 | ⇒コミュニティ |
| 知覚 | perception |
| 知覚的体制化 | perceptual organization |
| 知識 | knowledge |
| 知性化 | intellectualization |
| 知的障害 | intellectual disability |
| 知能 | intelligence |
| 知能検査 | intelligence test／IQ test |
| 知能指数 | intelligence quotient（IQ） |
| チーム・ティーチング | team teaching |
| チャンク | chunk |
| 注意 | attention |
| 注意欠陥多動性障害 | attention-deficit hyperactivity disorder（ADHD） |
| 注意集中困難 | inattention |
| 注意の範囲 | span of attention |
| 中央値 | ⇒メディアン |
| 仲介変数 | intervening variable → mediating variable |
| 中心窩 | fovea |
| 中心化傾向 | central tendency |
| 中心視 | central vision |
| 中枢神経系 | central nervous system（CNS） |
| 中毒 | addiction |
| 中胚葉型 | mesomorphy |
| 中立性 | neutrality |
| 聴覚 | audition／auditory sense／sense of hearing |

# ちょうききおく

| | |
|---|---|
| 長期記憶 | long-term memory |
| 調整法 | method of adjustment |
| 丁度可知差異 | ⇒弁別閾 |
| 聴力障害 | hearing impairment |
| 直面化 | ⇒対決 |
| （論文）著者 | author |
| 直観像 | eidetic image |
| 治療 | treatment |
| 治療過程 | process of therapy |
| 治療構造 | therapeutic structure |
| 治療者 | ⇒セラピスト |
| 治療同盟 | therapeutic alliance |
| 沈黙 | silence |
| 沈黙の螺旋(らせん) | spiral of silence |
| 追従 | ⇒迎合 |
| 月の錯視 | moon illusion |
| 爪かみ（症） | nail biting |
| 出会い | ⇒エンカウンター |
| 出会い集団 | ⇒エンカウンター・グループ |
| 定位 | ⇒局在 |
| 定間隔強化 | fixed interval (FI) reinforcement |
| Tグループ | training group |
| $t$ 検定 | $t$-test |
| 抵抗 | resistance |
| ディセプション | deception |
| ディブリーフィング | debriefing |
| 定率強化スケジュール | fixed ratio (FR) schedule |
| 手がかり | cue |
| 敵意 | hostility |
| 適応 | adaptation／adjustment |
| 適応度 | fitness |

|  |  |
|---|---|
| 適合 | congruence |
| 適性 | aptitude |
| 適性検査 | aptitude test |
| 適性処遇交互作用 | aptitude treatment interaction (ATI) |
| テスト・再テスト法 | ⇒再検査法 |
| テストバッテリー | test battery → battery |
| テスト不安 | test anxiety |
| データ | data |
| データ駆動型処理 | data driven processing |
| 手続き | procedure |
| 手続記憶 | procedural memory |
| 手続的公正 | procedural justice |
| 手続的知識 | procedural knowledge |
| 徹底操作 | working through |
| デマ | demagogy |
| 転移 | transference |
| 転移精神病 | transference psychosis |
| てんかん | epilepsy |
| 転換症状 | conversion symptom |
| 天井効果 | ceiling effect |
| 展望的記憶 | prospective memory |
| 電話相談 | telephone counseling |
| 同一化 | identification |
| 同一視 | identification |
| 同一性 | ⇒アイデンティティ |
| 同一性拡散 | identity diffusion |
| 同一性危機 | identity crisis |
| 同一性障害 | identity disorder |
| 動因 | drive |
| 投影 | projection |

## とうえいせいどういつし

| | |
|---|---|
| 投影性同一視 | projective identification |
| 投映法 | ⇒投影法 |
| 投影法 | projective technique |
| 同化 | assimilation |
| 等価刺激 | equivalent stimulus |
| 動機 | motive |
| 動機づけ | motivation |
| 道具的条件づけ | instrumental conditioning |
| 統計検定力 | statistical power |
| 同型論 | isomorphism |
| 等現間隔法 | method of equal-appearing intervals |
| 瞳孔(どうこう) | pupil |
| 統合教育 | integration |
| 登校恐怖症 | school phobia |
| 登校拒否 | school refusal |
| 統合失調症 | schizophrenia |
| 統合失調症の | schizophrenic |
| 統合する | integrate |
| 統語解析 | syntactic parsing |
| 統語論 | syntax |
| 動作性検査 | performance test |
| 動作性知能 | performance intelligence |
| 洞察 | insight |
| 投射 | projection |
| 同性愛 | homosexuality |
| 統制群 | control group |
| 統制の所在 | ⇒ローカス・オブ・コントロール |
| 同調 | conformity |
| 頭頂葉 | parietal lobe |
| 動的家族描画法 | kinetic family drawings（KFD） |

|  |  |
|---|---|
| 道徳（性） | moral |
| 頭部叩き | head banging |
| 動物行動学 | ⇒比較行動学 |
| トゥレット障害 | Tourette's disorder／Gilles de la Tourette's syndrome |
| 特異的発達障害 | specific developmental disorder (SDD) |
| 読字障害 | dyslexia |
| 特殊学級 | special class |
| 特性論 | trait theory |
| 得点化 | ⇒スコアリング |
| 独立 | independence |
| 独立変数 | independent variable |
| トークン・エコノミー | token economy |
| 度数 | frequency |
| 度数分布 | frequency distribution |
| トップダウン処理 | top-down processing |
| ドーパミン | dopamine (DA) |
| トラウマ | trauma |
| 取り入り | ⇒迎合 |
| 取り入れ | introjection |
| 取り込み | ⇒取り入れ |
| トリックスター | trickster |
| ドリーム・ワーク | dream work |

## な 行

|  |  |
|---|---|
| 内因性の | endogenous ⟷ exogenous |
| 内観 | introspection |
| 内言 | ⇒内語 |
| 内言語 | ⇒内語 |
| 内語 | inner speech |

| | |
|---|---|
| 内向性 | introversion ⟵⟶ extraversion |
| 内在化 | internalization ⟵⟶ externalization |
| 内集団びいき | in-group favoritism |
| 内制止 | internal inhibition |
| 内的言語 | ⇒内語 |
| 内的作業モデル | internal working model（IWM） |
| 内的整合性 | internal consistency |
| 内的妥当性 | internal validity |
| 内胚葉型 | endomorphy |
| 内発的動機づけ | intrinsic motivation ⟵⟶ extrinsic motivation |
| 内罰的反応 | intropunitive response |
| 内部感覚 | internal sense |
| ナイーブな参加者 | naive participant ⟵⟶ confederate |
| 内分泌 | internal secretion |
| 内分泌腺 | endocrine gland |
| 内包 | connotation |
| 内容的妥当性 | content validity |
| なぐり描き | scribble ／ squiggle |
| ナルコレプシー | narcolepsy |
| ナルシシズム | narcissism |
| 慣れ | habituation |
| なわばり | territory |
| 喃語 | babbling |
| 二項分布 | binomial distribution |
| 二重拘束 | ⇒ダブルバインド |
| 二重ブラインドテスト | double blind test |
| 二重盲検法（二重遮蔽法） | double blind test |
| 日内変動 | diurnal variation |
| 日周期リズム | circadian rhythm |
| 乳児期 | infancy |

| | |
|---|---|
| 入力 | input |
| ニューラル・ネットワーク | neural network |
| ニューロン | neuron |
| 二卵性双生児 | fraternal twins |
| 人間―機械系 | man-machine system |
| 人間工学 | ergonomics / human engineering |
| 人間性心理学 | humanistic psychology |
| 人間中心セラピー | ⇒パーソン・センタード・アプローチ |
| 認知 | cognition |
| 認知機能 | cognitive function |
| 認知機能障害 | cognitive dysfunction |
| 認知行動療法 | cognitive behavioral therapy |
| 認知症 | dementia |
| 認知心理学 | cognitive psychology |
| 認知斉合性 | cognitive consistency |
| 認知地図 | cognitive map |
| 認知的制約 | cognitive constraint |
| 認知的評価 | cognitive appraisal |
| 認知の不協和 | cognitive dissonance |
| 認知プロセス | cognitive process |
| 年齢級の | age graded |
| 脳炎 | encephalitis |
| 脳器質症候群 | brain organic syndrome |
| 脳磁図 | magnetoencephalogram (MEG) |
| 脳性麻痺 | cerebral palsy (CP) |
| 能動的想像 | ⇒アクティブ・イマジネーション |
| 脳波 | brain waves / electroencephalogram (EEG) |
| 脳波計 | electroencephalograph |
| 能率 | ⇒効率 |
| 能力 | ability |

| | |
|---|---|
| ノーマリゼーション | normalization |
| ノルアドレナリン | noradrenaline (NA) → norepinephrine |
| ノルエピネフリン | norepinephrine (NE) → noradrenaline |
| ノンバーバル・コミュニケーション | non-verbal communication (NVC) |
| ノンパラメトリック検定法 | nonparametric test → nonparametric method |
| ノンパラメトリック法 | nonparametric method → nonparametric test |
| ノンレム | non-rapid eye movement (non-REM) |
| ノンレム睡眠 | non-rapid eye movement sleep (NREM sleep) |

## は 行

| | |
|---|---|
| 場 | field |
| 把握反射 | grasping reflex |
| バイアス | bias |
| バイオフィードバック | biofeedback |
| 媒介変数 | mediating variable → intervening variable |
| 場依存性 | field dependence |
| ハイリスク乳幼児 | high risk infant |
| バウムテスト | Baumtest (独)／tree drawing test |
| 破壊性 | destructiveness |
| 破壊性行動障害 | disruptive behavior disorder |
| 破瓜型統合失調症（破瓜病） | hebephrenia |
| 白日夢 | ⇒白昼夢 |
| 剥奪 | deprivation |
| 白昼夢 | day dream |

| | |
|---|---|
| 箱庭療法 | sand play technique |
| 恥 | shame |
| パス解析 | path analysis |
| バズ・セッション | buzz session |
| パーソナリティ | personality |
| パーソナル・コミュニケーション | personal communication |
| パーソナル・スペース | personal space |
| パーソン・センタード・アプローチ | person-centered approach |
| 発生認識論 | genetic epistemology |
| 発達 | development |
| 発達加速現象 | developmental acceleration |
| 発達課題 | developmental task |
| 発達指数 | developmental quotient（DQ） |
| 発達障害 | developmental disorder |
| 発達性書字障害 | developmental dysgraphia |
| 発達性読字障害 | developmental reading disorder |
| 発達段階 | developmental stage |
| バッテリー | battery → test battery |
| 発話 | utterance |
| パニック | panic |
| パニック障害 | panic disorder |
| 母親語 | ⇒マザリーズ |
| バビンスキー反射 | Babinski reflex |
| 場面緘黙 | selective mutism |
| パラダイム | paradigm |
| パラノイア | paranoia |
| バリマックス回転 | varimax rotation |
| 場理論 | field theory |
| ハロー効果 | halo effect |
| バーンアウト | burnout |

| | |
|---|---|
| 般化 | generalization |
| 反抗挑戦性障害 | oppositional defiant disorder |
| 犯罪心理学 | criminological psychology |
| 反射 | reflex |
| 反社会的行動 | antisocial behavior |
| 反社会的人格 | antisocial personality |
| 反動形成 | reaction formation |
| 反応 | reaction／response |
| 反応時間 | reaction time |
| 反応する | respond |
| 反応性精神病 | reactive psychosis |
| 反応ポテンシャル | reaction potential |
| 反復強迫 | repetition compulsion |
| 反復測定のある分散分析 | repeated measures analysis of variance |
| 判別分析 | discriminant analysis |
| ピア・カウンセリング | peer counseling |
| PFスタディ | Picture-Frustration Study |
| PM理論 | PM theory |
| 比較行動学 | ethology |
| 比較心理学 | comparative psychology |
| 被虐待児症候群 | abused-child syndrome |
| 非急速眼球運動 | ⇒ノンレム |
| ピグマリオン効果 | Pygmalion effect |
| 非言語性（の） | non-verbal |
| 非言語的 | ⇒非言語性（の） |
| 非言語的コミュニケーション | ⇒ノンバーバル・コミュニケーション |
| 被検査者 | test taker／testee |
| 被験者 | subject → participant |
| 被験者間要因 | between-subject factor |
| 被験者内要因 | within-subject factor |

|  |  |
|---|---|
| 非行 | delinquency |
| 非公式集団 | ⇒インフォーマル・グループ |
| 微細脳機能障害 | Minimal Brain Dysfunction (MBD) |
| 非指示的カウンセリング | non-directive counseling |
| 皮質 | cortex |
| 微視的行動 | microscopic behavior<br>⟷ macroscopic behavior<br>→ molecular behavior |
| 非社会的行動 | asocial behavior |
| 比尺度 | ratio scale |
| ヒステリー | hysteria |
| ヒステリー性人格 | hysterical personality |
| 否定的感情 | negative emotion<br>⟷ positive emotion |
| (生物としての) ヒト | human beings |
| 人見知り | fear of stranger／stranger anxiety |
| ヒト免疫不全ウィルス | Human Immunodeficiency Virus (HIV) |
| 否認 | denial |
| 皮膚感覚 | cutaneous sense |
| 皮膚電気反応 | electrodermal response (EDR)／galvanic skin response (GSR) |
| 肥満症 | obesity |
| 秘密保持 | confidentiality |
| ヒューリスティック | heuristic |
| 憑依現象 | phenomenon of possession |
| 表意文字 | ideogram |
| 表音文字 | phonogram |
| 表現 | expression |
| 表現型 | phenotype ⟷ genotype |
| 病識 | insight into disease |

# ひょうしゅつ

| | |
|---|---|
| 表出 | expression |
| 標準化 | standardization |
| 標準化された | standardized |
| 標準偏差 | standard deviation ($SD$) |
| 表象 | representation |
| 表情 | facial expression |
| 病跡学 | pathography |
| 病前の | premorbid |
| （論文）表題 | ⇒タイトル |
| 病態水準 | level of psychopathology |
| 評定尺度 | rating scale |
| 評定法 | rating method |
| 平等にただよう注意 | free-floating attention |
| 標本 | ⇒サンプル |
| 標本抽出 | ⇒サンプリング |
| 比率の差の検定 | test of proportion |
| 比例尺度 | ⇒比尺度 |
| 疲労 | fatigue |
| 広場恐怖 | agoraphobia |
| 頻度 | frequency |
| 5-HT | ⇒セロトニン |
| ファシリテーション | facilitation |
| 不安 | anxiety／fear |
| 不安障害 | anxiety disorder |
| 不安神経症 | anxiety neurosis |
| 不一致 | incongruence |
| フィードバック | feedback |
| フィールド実験 | field experiment |
| フィンガーペインティング | finger painting |
| 風景構成法 | landscape montage technique |

| 夫婦カウンセリング | marital counseling |
| --- | --- |
| フェイスシート | face sheet |
| フェヒナーの法則 | Fechner's law |
| フェミニスト・セラピー | feminist therapy |
| フォーカシング | focusing |
| フォーマル・グループ | formal group ⟷ informal group |
| フォローアップ | follow-up |
| 不協和 | dissonance |
| 復号化 | decoding ⟷ encoding |
| 副交感神経系 | parasympathetic nervous system (PNS) |
| 服従 | obedience |
| 副腎皮質刺激ホルモン | adrenocorticotropic hormone (ACTH) |
| 輻輳（運動） | convergence |
| 符号化 | coding / encoding ⟷ decoding |
| 符号解読 | ⇒復号化 |
| 符号化する | ⇒コード化する |
| 父性 | fatherhood / paternity |
| 父性的干渉主義 | paternalism |
| 布置 | constellation |
| 不調和 | incongruence |
| 物心二元論 | dualism |
| 地理的環境 | geographical environment |
| 物理的な | physical |
| 不定愁訴 | unidentified complaints |
| 不適応 | maladjustment |
| 不適合 | incongruence |
| 不登校 | non-attendance at school |
| 負の | negative ⟷ positive |
| 不眠症 | insomnia |

| | |
|---|---|
| ブーメラン効果 | boomerang effect |
| プライマリ・ケア | primary care |
| プライミング | priming |
| ブラインド・アナリシス | blind analysis |
| プラシーボ | placebo |
| フラストレーション | frustration |
| プラセボ | ⇒プラシーボ |
| プラトー現象 | plateau phenomenon |
| ふり遊び | pretend play |
| フリースクール | free school |
| ブリーフセラピー | brief therapy |
| ふるい分け | ⇒スクリーニング |
| ブレインストーミング | brain storming |
| ブローカ領域 | Broca's area |
| プロスペクト理論 | prospect theory |
| プロトコル | protocol |
| プロフィール | profile |
| プロマックス回転 | promax rotation |
| 分化 | differentiation |
| 文化共通の | culture-general |
| 文化特異の | culture-specific |
| 分散 | variance |
| 分散分析 | analysis of variance (ANOVA) |
| 分子的行動 | molecular behavior<br>　　⟷ molar behavior<br>　　→ microscopic behavior |
| 文章完成法テスト | Sentence Completion Test (SCT) |
| 分配的公正 | distributive justice |
| 分布 | distribution |
| 文法 | grammar |
| 文脈 | context |

|  |  |
|---|---|
| 文理解 | sentence comprehension |
| 分離—個体化理論 | separation-individuation theory |
| 分離脳 | split brain |
| 分離不安 | separation anxiety |
| 分類 | classification |
| 分裂 | splitting |
| 平均値 | mean $(M)$ / average |
| 平衡感覚 | vestibular sense |
| 並行面接 | concomitant interview |
| 米国精神医学会 | American Psychiatric Association (APA) |
| ベイズ理論 | Bayes' theorem |
| 並列処理 | parallel processing |
| 並列分散処理 | parallel distributed processing |
| ベーシック・エンカウンターグループ | basic encounter group |
| ベータ波 | beta wave |
| ペニス羨望 | penis envy |
| ペルソナ | persona |
| 偏見 | prejudice |
| 変数 | variable |
| 偏頭痛 | migraine |
| 偏相関係数 | partial correlation coefficient |
| ベンダー・ゲシュタルト検査（テスト） | Bender Gestalt Test (BGT) / Bender Visual Motor Gestalt Test |
| 扁桃体 | amygdala |
| 弁別 | discrimination |
| 弁別閾 | differential limen (DL) / deference threshold / discriminative threshold just noticeable difference |
| 弁別刺激 | discriminative stimulus |

| | |
|---|---|
| 弁別的妥当性 | discriminant validity ／ divergent validity |
| 片麻痺(へんまひ) | hemiplegia |
| 防衛機制 | defense mechanism |
| 妨害刺激 | distracter |
| 包括的適応度 | inclusive fitness |
| 傍観者効果 | bystander effect |
| 忘却 | forgetting |
| 報酬 | reward |
| 方法 | method |
| 訪問面接 | visiting counseling |
| 方略 | strategy |
| 母語 | native language |
| 母子関係 | mother-child relationship |
| 母子固着 | mother-infant fixation |
| ポジション | position |
| 母子相互作用 | mother-infant interaction |
| ポジティブ・イリュージョン | positive illusion |
| 母子分離 | maternal separation |
| 母集団 | population |
| 補償 | compensation |
| 補色 | complementary colors |
| ホスピス | hospice |
| ホスピタリズム | hospitalism |
| 母性 | maternity ／ motherhood |
| 母性剥奪(はくだつ) | ⇒マターナル・ディプリベーション |
| 保続 | perseveration |
| 保存 | conservation |
| ホーソン研究 | Hawthorne study |
| ボーダーレス・ソサイエティ | borderless society |
| 没個性化 | deindividuation |

| | |
|---|---|
| ボディ・ランゲージ | body language |
| ボトムアップ処理 | bottom-up processing |
| ほどよい母親 | good enough mother |
| ホメオスタシス | homeostasis |
| ボランティア活動 | volunteer activity |
| ホールディング | holding |
| 本当の自己 | ⇒真の自己 |
| 本能 | instinct |
| 本能行動 | instinctive behavior |

## ま 行

| | |
|---|---|
| マイノリティ | minority ⟷ majority |
| マキャベリ的知能 | Machiavellian intelligence |
| マグニチュード推定法 | method of magnitude estimation |
| マザリーズ | motherese |
| マザリング | mothering |
| マジック・ミラー | one-way mirror |
| マジョリティ | majority ⟷ minority |
| マスキング | masking |
| マゾヒズム | masochism ⟷ sadism |
| マターナル・ディプリベーション | maternal deprivation |
| マルコフ連鎖 | Markov chain |
| 味覚 | gustation／gustatory sense／sense of taste |
| 未熟児 | premature infant |
| 見捨てられ不安 | abandonment anxiety |
| 見通し | insight |
| ミネソタ多面人格目録 | Minnesota Multiphasic Personality Inventory (MMPI) |
| 身振り語 | ⇒ボディ・ランゲージ |
| 民話 | folktale |

# むいしき

| | |
|---|---|
| 無意識（の） | unconscious |
| 無関心 | ⇒アパシー |
| 無感動 | ⇒アパシー |
| 無気力 | apathy → helplessness |
| 無作為抽出 | ⇒ランダム抽出 |
| 無条件刺激 | unconditioned stimulus |
| 無条件の肯定的関心 | unconditional positive regard |
| 夢中遊行症 | sleep-walking |
| 無罰的反応 | impunitive response |
| 夢遊病 | ⇒夢中遊行症 |
| 無力感 | helplessness → apathy |
| 明暗順応 | light and dark adaptation |
| 名義尺度 | nominal scale |
| 明順応 | light adaptation |
| 瞑想 | meditation |
| 命題 | proposition |
| 命題表象 | propositional representation |
| 迷路 | maze |
| 目かくし分析 | ⇒ブラインド・アナリシス |
| メタアンフェタミン | methamphetamine → amphetamine |
| メタ記憶 | metamemory |
| メタ認知 | metacognition |
| メタ分析 | meta-analysis |
| メディアリテラシー | media literacy |
| メディアン | median |
| メランコリー | melancholia |
| メランコリー親和型性格 | melancholic type |
| 面接 | interview |
| 妄想 | delusion |
| 妄想症 | ⇒パラノイア |

| | |
|---|---|
| 妄想分裂態勢 | ⇒妄想分裂ポジション |
| 妄想分裂ポジション | paranoid-schizoid position |
| 網膜 | retina |
| 燃え尽き | ⇒バーンアウト |
| モーガンの公準 | Morgan's Canon |
| 黙従傾向 | ⇒イエス・テンデンシー |
| (研究) 目的 | purpose／aim |
| 目標 | goal |
| 目標勾配 | goal gradient |
| 目標刺激 | target |
| 目標指向行動 | goal directed behavior |
| 目標達成への意欲 | ⇒モラール |
| 目録 | inventory |
| モジュラリティ | modularity |
| モーズレイ性格検査 | Maudsley Personality Inventory (MPI) → Eysenck Personality Questionnaire |
| モダリティ | modality → sense modality |
| モッブ | mob |
| モデリング | modeling |
| モード | mode |
| 喪の仕事 | mourning work |
| 模倣 | imitation |
| モラトリアム | moratorium |
| モラール | morale |
| モル的行動 | molar behavior ⟷ molecular behavior → macroscopic behavior |
| モロー反射 | Moro reflex |
| 問題解決 | problem solving |
| 問題行動 | problematic behavior |

## や行

| | |
|---|---|
| 野 | field |
| 野外実験 | ⇒フィールド実験 |
| 夜間徘徊 | night walking |
| 夜驚 | night terror ／ nightmare ／ sleep terror |
| 夜尿症 | nocturnal enuresis |
| やり取り遊び | alternating play |
| 有意水準 | level of significance |
| (統計的に) 有意な | significant |
| 誘因 | incentive |
| 優越コンプレックス | superiority complex ⟷ inferiority complex |
| 遊戯療法 | play therapy |
| 誘導 | induction |
| 誘導運動 | induced movement |
| 誘発電位 | evoked potential |
| 有病率 | prevalence |
| 床効果 | floor effect |
| 歪み | ⇒バイアス |
| ユース・カルチャー | youth culture |
| 指しゃぶり | finger sucking |
| ユーモア | humor |
| 養育 | nurture ／ parenting |
| 要因 | factor |
| 要因計画 | factorial design |
| 要求 | need |
| 要求水準 | level of aspiration |
| 幼児期 | early childhood |
| 幼児性欲 | infantile sexuality |

| | |
|---|---|
| 陽性転移 | positive transference ⟷ negative transference |
| 幼稚症 | infantilism |
| (論文) 要約 | ⇒アブストラクト |
| 予期不安 | anticipatory anxiety |
| 抑圧 | repression |
| 抑圧する | repress |
| 抑うつ | depression |
| 抑うつ神経症 | depressive neurosis |
| 抑制 | inhibition / suppression |
| 抑制する | inhibit / suppress |
| 欲動 | drive |
| 予後 | prognosis |
| 予測 | prediction |
| 予測的妥当性 | predictive validity |
| 欲求 | need |
| 欲求階層 (説) | hierarchy of needs |
| 欲求不満 | ⇒フラストレーション |
| 欲求不満耐性 | frustration tolerance |
| 読み | reading |

## ら 行

| | |
|---|---|
| 来談者 | ⇒クライエント |
| 来談者中心療法 | client-centered therapy |
| 楽観的な幻想 | optimistic illusion |
| ラベリング | labeling |
| ラポート | ⇒ラポール |
| ラポール | rapport |
| 乱衆 | ⇒モッブ |
| ランダム抽出 | random sampling |

## りがくりょうほう

| | |
|---|---|
| 理学療法 | physical therapy (PT) ／ physiotherapy |
| リカート尺度 | Likert scale |
| リクリエーション療法 | recreational therapy |
| 離婚 | divorce |
| 離人症 | depersonalization |
| リスク | risk |
| 理想化 | idealization |
| リーダーシップ | leadership |
| 利他主義 | altruism |
| 立体視 | stereopsis ／ stereoscopic vision |
| 里程標 | milestone |
| リテラシー | literacy |
| リハビリテーション | rehabilitation |
| リビドー（論） | libido |
| リフレーミング | reframing |
| 流言 | rumor |
| 流行 | fashion |
| 流動性知能 | fluid intelligence |
| 領域 | ⇒野 |
| 両価性 | ⇒アンビバレンス |
| 両眼視 | binocular vision |
| 両眼視差 | binocular disparity |
| 両性具有 | androgyny |
| 両側性転移 | bilateral transfer |
| 両面価値 | ⇒アンビバレンス |
| 両面感情 | ⇒アンビバレンス |
| リラクセーション | relaxation |
| 臨界期 | critical period |
| 臨死体験 | near death experience |
| 倫理綱領 | ethical principles |

| | |
|---|---|
| 類型論 | type theory |
| 類推 | analogy |
| 累積度数 | cumulative frequency |
| レッテル貼り | ⇒ラベリング |
| 劣等感 | inferiority feeling |
| 劣等コンプレックス | inferiority complex<br>⟵⟶ superiority complex |
| レファレンス・グループ | reference group |
| レム | rapid eye movement（REM） |
| 連合 | association |
| 連想 | association |
| 連続強化 | continuous reinforcement |
| 老化 | ⇒エイジング |
| 老賢者 | wise old man |
| 老年学 | gerontology |
| ローカス・オブ・コントロール | locus of control |
| ロールシャッハ・テスト | Rorschach Test |
| ロールプレイ | role play |

## わ 行

| | |
|---|---|
| ワーカホリック | workaholic |
| 若者文化 | ⇒ユース・カルチャー |
| ワーキングメモリー | working memory |
| ワークショップ | workshop |
| われわれ意識 | we-consciousness |

# 人名集
## アルファベット→カタカナ

※生誕年，没年が非公開である場合は―で示した。

## A

| | | | |
|---|---|---|---|
| Adler, Alfred | アドラー, A. | 1870〜1937 | J |
| Ainsworth, Mary D. S. | エインズワース, M. D. S. | 1913〜1999 | H |
| Allport, Floyd H. | オルポート, F. H. | 1890〜1978 | I |
| Allport, Gordon W. | オルポート, G. W. | 1897〜1967 | G |
| Anderson, John R. | アンダーソン, J. R. | 1947〜 | D |
| Argyle, Michael | アーガイル, M. | 1925〜2002 | I |
| Aristotle | アリストテレス | B.C. 384〜322 | A |
| Aronson, Elliot | アロンソン, E. | 1932〜 | I |
| Asch, Solomon E. | アッシュ, S. E. | 1907〜1996 | I |
| Atkinson, John W. | アトキンソン, J. W. | 1923〜2003 | F G |
| Atkinson, Richard C. | アトキンソン, R. C. | 1929〜 | F |
| Ausubel, David P. | オーズベル, D. P. | 1918〜2008 | H |
| Axline, Virginia M. | アクスライン, V. M. | 1911〜1988 | J |

## B

| | | | |
|---|---|---|---|
| Baddeley, Alan D. | バッドリー（バドリー）, A. D. | 1934〜 | D |
| Baldwin, James M. | ボールドウィン, J. M. | 1861〜1934 | A H I |
| Bandura, Albert | バンデューラ, A. | 1925〜 | I |
| Beck, Aaron T. | ベック, A. T. | 1921〜 | J |
| Bem, Daryl J. | ベム, D. J. | 1938〜 | F G I |
| Bem, Sandra L. | ベム, S. L. | 1944〜2014 | G I |
| Benedict, Ruth F. | ベネディクト, R. F. | 1887〜1948 | I |

| | | | |
|---|---|---|---|
| Berne, Eric | バーン, E. | 1910～1970 | J |
| Binet, Alfred | ビネー, A. | 1857～1911 | G |
| Blos, Peter | ブロス, P. | 1904～1997 | H J |
| Bower, Thomas G. R. | バウアー, T. G. R. | 1941～2014 | B H |
| Bowlby, John | ボウルビィ, J. | 1907～1990 | H |
| Broca, P. Paul | ブローカ（ブロッカー）, P. P. | 1824～1880 | B |
| Bronfenbrenner, Urie | ブロンフェンブレンナー, U. | 1917～2005 | H |
| Bruner, Jerome S. | ブルーナー, J. S. | 1915～2016 | B C D H |
| Bühler, Charlotte | ビューラー, C. | 1893～1974 | H |
| Bühler, Karl | ビューラー, K. | 1879～1963 | H |
| Byrne, Donn | バーン, D. | 1931～2014 | G I |

## C

| | | | |
|---|---|---|---|
| Cannon, Walter B. | キャノン, W. B. | 1871～1945 | B F |
| Cartwright, Dorwin P. | カートライト, D. P. | 1915～2008 | I |
| Cattell, James M. | キャッテル, J. M. | 1860～1944 | A |
| Cattell, Raymond B. | キャッテル, R. B. | 1905～1998 | G I |
| Charcot, Jean M. | シャルコー, J. M. | 1825～1893 | A J |
| Chomsky, Avram N. | チョムスキー, A. N. | 1928～ | E |
| Cialdini, Robert B. | チャルディーン（チャルディーニ）, R. B. | 1945～ | I |
| Cloward, Richard A. | クラワード, R. A. | 1926～2001 | J |
| Cochran, William G. | コクラン, W. G. | 1909～1980 | K |
| Cohen, Albert K. | コーエン, A. K. | 1918～2014 | J |
| Cooley, Charles H. | クーリー, C. H. | 1864～1929 | I |
| Cox, Gertrude M. | コックス, G. M. | 1900～1978 | K |
| Cressey, Donald R. | クレッシー, D. R. | 1919～1987 | J |
| Cronbach, Lee J. | クロンバック（クロンバッハ), L. J. | 1916～2001 | K |

## D

| | | | |
|---|---|---|---|
| Darwin, Charles | ダーウィン, C. | 1809〜1882 | A H |
| Dawkins, Richard | ドーキンス, R. | 1941〜 | C |
| Deci, Edward L. | ディシ (デシ), E. L. | 1942〜 | C F I |
| Descartes, René | デカルト, R. | 1596〜1650 | A |
| Deutsch, Morton | ドイッチュ, M. | 1920〜2017 | J |
| Dewey, John | デューイ, J. | 1859〜1952 | A |
| Dumas, Georges | デュマ, G. | 1866〜1946 | A |

## E

| | | | |
|---|---|---|---|
| Ebbinghaus, Hermann | エビングハウス, H. | 1850〜1909 | D |
| Eisenberg, Nancy | アイゼンバーグ, N. | — | H |
| Ekman, Paul | エクマン, P. | 1934〜 | F |
| Ellis, Albert | エリス, A. | 1913〜2007 | J |
| Erikson, Erik H. | エリクソン, E. H. | 1902〜1994 | G |
| Eysenck, Hans J. | アイゼンク, H. J. | 1916〜1997 | B G J |

## F

| | | | |
|---|---|---|---|
| Fantz, Robert L. | ファンツ, R. L. | 1925〜1981 | H |
| Fechner, Gustav T. | フェヒナー, G. T. | 1801〜1887 | A B |
| Festinger, Leon | フェスティンガー (フェスティンジャー), L. | 1919〜1989 | I |
| Fisher, Ronald A. | フィッシャー, R. A. | 1890〜1962 | K |
| Frankl, Viktor E. | フランクル, V. E. | 1905〜1997 | J |
| Freud, Anna | フロイト, A. | 1895〜1982 | J |
| Freud, Sigmund | フロイト, S. | 1856〜1939 | J |
| Froebel, Friedrich W. A. | フレーベル, F. W. A. | 1782〜1852 | H |
| Fromm, Erich | フロム, E. | 1900〜1980 | I J |

## G

| | | | |
|---|---|---|---|
| Gall, Franz J. | ガル, F. J. | 1758〜1828 | A B |
| Galton, Sir Francis | ゴールトン, S. F. | 1822〜1911 | A G K |
| Gesell, Arnold L. | ゲゼル, A. L. | 1880〜1961 | H |
| Gibson, Eleanor J. | ギブソン, E. J. | 1910〜2002 | B |
| Gibson, James J. | ギブソン, J. J. | 1904〜1979 | B |
| Glaser, Daniel | グレーサー(グレーザー), D. | ― | J |
| Glueck, Eleanor | グリュック, E. | 1898〜1972 | J |
| Glueck, Sheldon | グリュック, S. | 1896〜1980 | J |
| Guilford, Joy P. | ギルフォード, J. P. | 1897〜1987 | G |
| Guttman, Louis | ガットマン, L. | 1916〜1987 | K |

## H

| | | | |
|---|---|---|---|
| Hall, Granville S. | ホール, G. S. | 1844〜1924 | A H |
| Hamilton, William D. | ハミルトン, W. D. | 1936〜2000 | A C H I |
| Harlow, Harry F. | ハーロウ, H. F. | 1905〜1981 | C H |
| Havighurst, Robert J. | ハヴィガースト, R. J. | 1900〜1991 | H |
| Healy, William | ヒーリー, W. | 1869〜1963 | J |
| Hebb, Donald O. | ヘッブ, D. O. | 1904〜1985 | B C |
| Heider, Fritz | ハイダー, F. | 1896〜1988 | I |
| Helmholtz, Hermann L. F. von | ヘルムホルツ, H. L. F. von | 1821〜1894 | A B |
| Hess, Eckhard H. | ヘス, E. H. | 1916〜1986 | B F I |
| Hilgard, Ernest R. | ヒルガード, E. R. | 1904〜2001 | C F |
| Hirschi, Travis | ハーシ, T. | 1935〜2017 | J |
| Holland, John L. | ホランド, J. L. | 1919〜2008 | G I |
| Horney, Karen | ホーナイ, K. | 1885〜1952 | H J |
| Hovland, Carl I. | ホブランド, C. I. | 1912〜1961 | E I |
| Hull, Clark L. | ハル, C. L. | 1884〜1952 | C |

## J

| | | | |
|---|---|---|---|
| James, William | ジェームズ, W. | 1842～1910 | A |
| Janet, Pierre | ジャネー, P. | 1859～1947 | J |
| Janis, Irving L. | ジャニス, I. L. | 1918～1990 | I |
| Jaspers, Karl | ヤスパース, K. | 1883～1969 | A |
| Jeffrey, Clarence R. | ジェフリー, C. R. | — | J |
| Jourard, Sidney M. | ジェラード (ジュラード), S. M. | 1926～1974 | J |
| Jung, Carl G. | ユング, C. G. | 1875～1961 | J |

## K

| | | | |
|---|---|---|---|
| Kagan, Jerome | ケーガン, J. | 1929～ | H |
| Kahneman, Daniel | カーネマン, D. | 1934～ | I |
| Kanner, Leo | カナー, L. | 1894～1981 | J |
| Kant, Immanuel | カント, I. | 1724～1804 | A |
| Kelley, Harold H. | ケリー, H. H. | 1921～2003 | I |
| Kelly, George A. | ケリー, G. A. | 1905～1967 | J |
| Kendall, Maurice G. | ケンドール, M. G. | 1907～1983 | K |
| Kernberg, Otto F. | カーンバーグ, O. F. | 1928～ | J |
| Klein, Melanie | クライン, M. | 1882～1960 | J |
| Koffka, Kurt | コフカ, K. | 1886～1941 | B C D H |
| Kohlberg, Lawrence | コールバーグ, L. | 1927～1987 | H |
| Köhler, Wolfgang | ケーラー, W. | 1887～1967 | C D |
| Kohut, Heinz | コフート, H. | 1913～1981 | J |
| Kraepelin, Emil | クレペリン, E. | 1856～1926 | J |
| Kretschmer, Ernst | クレッチマー, E. | 1888～1964 | J |
| Kruskal, William H. | クラスカル, W. H. | 1919～2005 | K |
| Kübler-Ross, Elisabeth | キューブラー・ロス, E. | 1926～2004 | J |

## L

| | | | |
|---|---|---|---|
| Lacan, Jacques | ラカン, J. | 1901〜1981 | A |
| Latané, Bibb | ラタネ, B. | 1937〜 | I |
| Lazarus, Richard S. | ラザルス, R. S. | 1922〜2002 | B F J |
| Leibniz, Gottfried W. von | ライプニッツ, G. W. von | 1646〜1716 | A |
| Levinson, Daniel J. | レヴィンソン, D. J. | 1920〜1994 | G |
| Lewin, Kurt | レヴィン, K. | 1890〜1947 | I |
| Likert, Rensis | リカート<br>(リッカート), R. | 1903〜1981 | K |
| Locke, John | ロック, J. | 1632〜1704 | A H |
| Loftus, Elizabeth F. | ロフタス, E. F. | 1944〜 | D I J |
| Lombroso, Cesare | ロンブローゾ, C. | 1836〜1909 | J |
| Lorenz, Konrad | ローレンツ, K. | 1903〜1989 | C |
| Luria, Alexander R. | ルリア, A. R. | 1902〜1977 | E |

## M

| | | | |
|---|---|---|---|
| Mahler, Margaret S. | マーラー, M. S. | 1897〜1985 | H J |
| Maslow, Abraham H. | マズロー<br>(マスロー), A. H. | 1908〜1970 | G |
| McClelland, David C. | マクレランド, D. C. | 1917〜1998 | F |
| McClelland, James L. | マクレランド, J. L. | 1948〜 | D |
| McDougall, William | マクドゥーガル, W. | 1871〜1938 | F C |
| McKay, Henry D. | マッケイ, H. D. | 1899〜1980 | J |
| McNemar, Quinn | マクネマー<br>(マックネマー), Q. | 1900〜1986 | K |
| Mead, George H. | ミード, G. H. | 1863〜1931 | I |
| Mead, Margaret | ミード, M. | 1901〜1978 | I |
| Mehrabian, Albert | メーラビアン<br>(メラビアン), A. | 1939〜 | F |
| Merton, Robert K. | マートン, R. K. | 1910〜2003 | I J |
| Milgram, Stanley | ミルグラム, S. | 1933〜1984 | I |

## Miller

| | | | |
|---|---|---|---|
| Miller, George A. | ミラー, G. A. | 1920～2012 | D E |
| Miller, Neal E. | ミラー, N. E. | 1909～2002 | C F |
| Montessori, Maria | モンテッソーリ, M. | 1870～1952 | H |
| Moreno, Jacob L. | モレノ, J. L. | 1892～1974 | J |
| Müller-Lyer, Franz C. | ミューラー・リヤー (ミュラー・リエル), F. C. | 1857～1916 | B |
| Murray, Henry A. | マーレー (マレー), H. A. | 1893～1988 | F J |

## N

| | | | |
|---|---|---|---|
| Neisser, Ulric | ナイサー, U. | 1928～2012 | B D |
| Newcomb, Theodore M. | ニューカム, T. M. | 1903～1984 | I |

## O

| | | | |
|---|---|---|---|
| Osgood, Charles E. | オズグッド, C. E. | 1916～1991 | K |

## P

| | | | |
|---|---|---|---|
| Parsons, Frank | パーソンズ, F. | 1854～1908 | H I J |
| Parsons, Talcott | パーソンズ, T. | 1902～1979 | A I |
| Pavlov, Ivan P. | パブロフ, I. P. | 1849～1936 | A |
| Pearson, Karl | ピアソン, K. | 1857～1936 | K |
| Penfield, Wilder G. | ペンフィールド, W. G. | 1891～1976 | B |
| Piaget, Jean | ピアジェ, J. | 1896～1980 | H |
| Plato | プラトン | B.C. 427～347 | A |
| Portmann, Adolf | ポルトマン, A. | 1897～1982 | H |
| Premack, David | プレマック, D. | 1925～2015 | C H |

## Q

| | | | |
|---|---|---|---|
| Quinney, Richard | クイニー, R. | 1934～ | J |

## R

| | | | |
|---|---|---|---|
| Rogers, Carl R. | ロジャーズ, C. R. | 1902〜1987 | J |
| Rorschach, Hermann | ロールシャッハ, H. | 1884〜1922 | J |
| Rosenberg, Morris J. | ローゼンバーグ, M. J. | 1922〜1992 | G I |
| Rosenthal, Robert | ローゼンサール<br>(ローゼンタール)<br>(ローゼンソール), R. | 1933〜 | I |
| Rosenzweig, Saul | ローゼンツワイク, S. | 1907〜2004 | F G J |
| Rotter, Julian B. | ロッター, J. B. | 1916〜2014 | C |
| Rousseau, Jean-Jacques | ルソー, J. | 1712〜1778 | A H |
| Rubin, Edgar J. | ルビン, E. J. | 1886〜1951 | A B |
| Rumelhart, David E. | ラメルハート<br>(ルーメルハート)<br>(ルメルハート), D. E. | 1942〜2011 | D |

## S

| | | | |
|---|---|---|---|
| Sameroff, Arnold J. | サメロフ, A. J. | — | H |
| Sartre, Jean-Paul | サルトル, J. | 1905〜1980 | A |
| Schachter, Stanley | シャクター, S. | 1922〜1997 | I |
| Schlosberg, Harold | シュロスバーグ, H. | 1904〜1964 | F |
| Schultz, Johannes H. | シュルツ, J. H. | 1884〜1970 | J |
| Seligman, Martin | セリグマン, M. | 1942〜 | B F I |
| Selye, Hans | セリエ, H. | 1907〜1982 | B |
| Shaw, Clifford R. | ショウ, C. R. | 1896〜1957 | J |
| Sheldon, William H. | シェルドン, W. H. | 1898〜1977 | G |
| Sherif, Muzafer | シェリフ, M. | 1906〜1988 | I |
| Singer, Margaret T. | シンガー, M. T. | 1921〜2003 | J |
| Skinner, Burrhus F. | スキナー, B. F. | 1904〜1990 | C |
| Spearman, Charles E. | スピアマン, C. E. | 1863〜1945 | K |
| Sperry, Roger W. | スペリー, R. W. | 1913〜1994 | B J |

| | | | |
|---|---|---|---|
| Spielberger, Charles D. | スピルバーガー, C. D. | 1927〜2013 | F |
| Spitz, René A. | スピッツ, R. A. | 1887〜1974 | H |
| Spranger, Eduard | シュプランガー, E. | 1882〜1963 | G I |
| Stern, Daniel N. | スターン, D. N. | 1934〜2012 | H J |
| Stern, William L. | シュテルン, W. L. | 1871〜1938 | A G H |
| Sternberg, Robert J. | スタンバーグ, R. J. | 1949〜 | G I |
| Stevens, Stanley S. | スティーブンス, S. S. | 1906〜1973 | B K |
| Sullivan, Harry S. | サリヴァン, H. S. | 1892〜1949 | J |
| Sutherland, Edwin H. | サザーランド (サザランド), E. H. | 1883〜1950 | J |

## T

| | | | |
|---|---|---|---|
| Tajfel, Henri | タジフェル, H. | 1919〜1982 | I |
| Terman, Lewis M. | ターマン, L. M. | 1877〜1956 | G |
| Tesser, Abraham | テッサー, A. | — | I J |
| Thorndike, Edward L. | ソーンダイク, E. L. | 1874〜1949 | C |
| Thurstone, Louis L. | サーストン, L. L. | 1887〜1955 | K |
| Tinbergen, Nikolaas | ティンバーゲン (ティンベルヘン), N. | 1907〜1988 | C |
| Titchener, Edward B. | ティチェナー (ティッチナー) (ティチナー), E. B. | 1867〜1927 | A |
| Tolman, Edward C. | トールマン, E. C. | 1886〜1959 | C |
| Tukey, John W. | テューキー, J. W. | 1915〜2000 | K |
| Tulving, Endel | タルヴィング (タルビング), E. | 1927〜 | D |

## V

| | | | |
|---|---|---|---|
| Vold, George B. | ヴォルド, G. B. | 1896〜1967 | J |
| Vygotsky, Lev S. | ヴィゴツキー, L. S. | 1896〜1934 | D H |

## W

| | | | |
|---|---|---|---|
| Wallis, Wilson A. | ウォーラス (ウォリス), W. A. | 1912〜1998 | K |
| Wallon, Henri P. H. | ワロン, H. P. H. | 1879〜1962 | H |
| Watson, John B. | ワトソン, J. B. | 1878〜1958 | C |
| Weber, Ernst H. | ウェーバー, E. H. | 1795〜1878 | B |
| Wechsler, David | ウェクスラー, D. | 1896〜1981 | G |
| Weiner, Bernard | ワイナー, B. | 1935〜 | I |
| Werner, Heinz | ウェルナー, H. | 1890〜1964 | H |
| Wernicke, Karl | ウェルニッケ, K. | 1848〜1905 | B |
| Wertheimer, Max | ヴェルトハイマー, M. | 1880〜1943 | B D |
| Whitney, Donald R. | ホイットニー, D. R. | 1915〜2007 | K |
| Wiener, Norbert | ウィーナー, N. | 1894〜1964 | B |
| Wilcoxon, Frank | ウィルコクソン, F. | 1892〜1965 | K |
| Winnicott, Donald W. | ウィニコット, D. W. | 1896〜1971 | H J |
| Witmer, Lightner | ウィットマー, L. | 1867〜1956 | J |
| Wolf, Christian | ウォルフ (ヴォルフ), C. | 1679〜1754 | A |
| Wolpe, Joseph | ウォルピ, J. | 1915〜1997 | J |
| Wundt, Wilhelm | ヴント, W. | 1832〜1920 | B |

## Y

| | | | |
|---|---|---|---|
| Yates, Frank | イェーツ (イエーツ), F. | 1902〜1994 | K |

## Z

| | | | |
|---|---|---|---|
| Zajonc, Robert B. | ザイアンス, R. B. | 1923〜2008 | D I |
| Zimbardo, Philip | ジンバルドー, P. | 1933〜 | I |

# 人名集
カタカナ→アルファベット

※生誕年，没年が非公開である場合は—で示した。

## あ 行

| | | | |
|---|---|---|---|
| アイゼンク, H. J. | Eysenck, Hans J. | 1916〜1997 | B G J |
| アイゼンバーグ, N. | Eisenberg, Nancy | — | H |
| アーガイル, M. | Argyle, Michael | 1925〜2002 | I |
| アクスライン, V. M. | Axline, Virginia M. | 1911〜1988 | J |
| アッシュ, S. E. | Asch, Solomon E. | 1907〜1996 | I |
| アトキンソン, J. W. | Atkinson, John W. | 1923〜2003 | F G |
| アトキンソン, R. C. | Atkinson, Richard C. | 1929〜 | F |
| アドラー, A. | Adler, Alfred | 1870〜1937 | J |
| アリストテレス | Aristotle | B.C. 384〜 322 | A |
| アロンソン, E. | Aronson, Elliot | 1932〜 | I |
| アンダーソン, J. R. | Anderson, John R. | 1947〜 | D |
| イェーツ, F. | Yates, Frank | 1902〜1994 | K |
| イエーツ, F. | ⇒イェーツ, F. | | |
| ヴィゴツキー, L. S. | Vygotsky, Lev S. | 1896〜1934 | D H |
| ウィットマー, L. | Witmer, Lightner | 1867〜1956 | J |
| ウィーナー, N. | Wiener, Norbert | 1894〜1964 | B |
| ウィニコット, D. W. | Winnicott, Donald W. | 1896〜1971 | H J |
| ウィルコクソン, F. | Wilcoxon, Frank | 1892〜1965 | K |
| ウェクスラー, D. | Wechsler, David | 1896〜1981 | G |
| ウェーバー, E. H. | Weber, Ernst H. | 1795〜1878 | B |
| ヴェルトハイマー, M. | Wertheimer, Max | 1880〜1943 | B D |
| ウェルナー, H. | Werner, Heinz | 1890〜1964 | H |

| ウェルニッケ, K. | Wernicke, Karl | 1848〜1905 | B |
|---|---|---|---|
| ウォーラス, W. A. | Wallis, Wilson A. | 1912〜1998 | K |
| ウォリス, W. A. | ⇒ウォーラス, W. A. | | |
| ヴォルド, G. B. | Vold, George B. | 1896〜1967 | J |
| ウォルピ, J. | Wolpe, Joseph | 1915〜1997 | J |
| ウォルフ, C. | Wolf, Christian | 1679〜1754 | A |
| ヴォルフ, C. | ⇒ウォルフ, C. | | |
| ヴント, W. | Wundt, Wilhelm | 1832〜1920 | B |
| エインズワース, M. D. S. | Ainsworth, Mary D. S. | 1913〜1999 | H |
| エクマン, P. | Ekman, Paul | 1934〜 | F |
| エビングハウス, H. | Ebbinghaus, Hermann | 1850〜1909 | D |
| エリクソン, E. H. | Erikson, Erik H. | 1902〜1994 | G |
| エリス, A. | Ellis, Albert | 1913〜2007 | J |
| オズグッド, C. E. | Osgood, Charles E. | 1916〜1991 | K |
| オーズベル, D. P. | Ausubel, David P. | 1918〜2008 | H |
| オルポート, F. H. | Allport, Floyd H. | 1890〜1978 | I |
| オルポート, G. W. | Allport, Gordon W. | 1897〜1967 | G |

## か 行

| ガットマン, L. | Guttman, Louis | 1916〜1987 | K |
|---|---|---|---|
| カートライト, D. P. | Cartwright, Dorwin P. | 1915〜2008 | I |
| カナー, L. | Kanner, Leo | 1894〜1981 | J |
| カーネマン, D. | Kahneman, Daniel | 1934〜 | I |
| ガル, F. J. | Gall, Franz J. | 1758〜1828 | AB |
| カント, I. | Kant, Immanuel | 1724〜1804 | A |
| カーンバーグ, O. F. | Kernberg, Otto F. | 1928〜 | J |
| ギブソン, E. J. | Gibson, Eleanor J. | 1910〜2002 | B |
| ギブソン, J. J. | Gibson, James J. | 1904〜1979 | B |
| キャッテル, J. M. | Cattell, James M. | 1860〜1944 | A |
| キャッテル, R. B. | Cattell, Raymond B. | 1905〜1998 | GI |

## キャノン

| | | | |
|---|---|---|---|
| キャノン, W. B. | Cannon, Walter B. | 1871〜1945 | B F |
| キューブラー・ロス, E. | Kübler-Ross, Elisabeth | 1926〜2004 | J |
| ギルフォード, J. P. | Guilford, Joy P. | 1897〜1987 | G |
| クイニー, R. | Quinney, Richard | 1934〜 | J |
| クーリー, C. H. | Cooley, Charles H. | 1864〜1929 | I |
| クライン, M. | Klein, Melanie | 1882〜1960 | J |
| クラスカル, W. H. | Kruskal, William H. | 1919〜2005 | K |
| クラワード, R. A. | Cloward, Richard A. | 1926〜2001 | J |
| グリュック, E. | Glueck, Eleanor | 1898〜1972 | J |
| グリュック, S. | Glueck, Sheldon | 1896〜1980 | J |
| グレーサー, D. | Glaser, Daniel | — | J |
| グレーザー, D. | ⇒グレーサー, D. | | |
| クレッシー, D. R. | Cressey, Donald R. | 1919〜1987 | J |
| クレッチマー, E. | Kretschmer, Ernst | 1888〜1964 | J |
| クレペリン, E. | Kraepelin, Emil | 1856〜1926 | J |
| クロンバック, L. J. | Cronbach, Lee J. | 1916〜2001 | K |
| クロンバッハ, L. J. | ⇒クロンバック, L. J. | | |
| ケーガン, J. | Kagan, Jerome | 1929〜 | H |
| ゲゼル, A. L. | Gesell, Arnold L. | 1880〜1961 | H |
| ケーラー, W. | Köhler, Wolfgang | 1887〜1967 | C D |
| ケリー, G. A. | Kelly, George A. | 1905〜1967 | J |
| ケリー, H. H. | Kelley, Harold H. | 1921〜2003 | I |
| ケンドール, M. G. | Kendall, Maurice G. | 1907〜1983 | K |
| コーエン, A. K. | Cohen, Albert K. | 1918〜2014 | J |
| コクラン, W. G. | Cochran, William G. | 1909〜1980 | K |
| コックス, G. M. | Cox, Gertrude M. | 1900〜1978 | K |
| コフカ, K. | Koffka, Kurt | 1886〜1941 | B C D H |
| コフート, H. | Kohut, Heinz | 1913〜1981 | J |
| ゴールトン, S. F. | Galton, Sir Francis | 1822〜1911 | A G K |
| コールバーグ, L. | Kohlberg, Lawrence | 1927〜1987 | H |

## さ 行

| | | | |
|---|---|---|---|
| ザイアンス, R. B. | Zajonc, Robert B. | 1923〜2008 | D I |
| サザーランド, E. H. | Sutherland, Edwin H. | 1883〜1950 | J |
| サザランド, E. H. | ⇒サザーランド, E. H. | | |
| サーストン, L. L. | Thurstone, Louis L. | 1887〜1955 | K |
| サメロフ, A. J. | Sameroff, Arnold J. | — | H |
| サリヴァン, H. S. | Sullivan, Harry S. | 1892〜1949 | J |
| サルトル, J. | Sartre, Jean-Paul | 1905〜1980 | A |
| ジェフリー, C. R. | Jeffrey, Clarence R. | — | J |
| ジェームズ, W. | James, William | 1842〜1910 | A |
| ジェラード, S. M. | Jourard, Sidney M. | 1926〜1974 | J |
| シェリフ, M. | Sherif, Muzafer | 1906〜1988 | I |
| シェルドン, W. H. | Sheldon, William H. | 1898〜1977 | G |
| シャクター, S. | Schachter, Stanley | 1922〜1997 | I |
| ジャニス, I. L. | Janis, Irving L. | 1918〜1990 | I |
| ジャネー, P. | Janet, Pierre | 1859〜1947 | J |
| シャルコー, J. M. | Charcot, Jean M. | 1825〜1893 | A J |
| シュテルン, W. L. | Stern, William L. | 1871〜1938 | A G H |
| シュプランガー, E. | Spranger, Eduard | 1882〜1963 | G I |
| ジュラード, S. M. | ⇒ジェラード, S. M. | | |
| シュルツ, J. H. | Schultz, Johannes H. | 1884〜1970 | J |
| シュロスバーグ, H. | Schlosberg, Harold | 1904〜1964 | F |
| ショウ, C. R. | Shaw, Clifford R. | 1896〜1957 | J |
| シンガー, M. T. | Singer, Margaret T. | 1921〜2003 | J |
| ジンバルドー, P. | Zimbardo, Philip | 1933〜 | I |
| スキナー, B. F. | Skinner, Burrhus F. | 1904〜1990 | C |
| スターン, D. N. | Stern, Daniel N. | 1934〜2012 | H J |
| スタンバーグ, R. J. | Sternberg, Robert J. | 1949〜 | G I |
| スティーブンス, S. S. | Stevens, Stanley S. | 1906〜1973 | B K |
| スピアマン, C. E. | Spearman, Charles E. | 1863〜1945 | K |

スピッツ

| | | | |
|---|---|---|---|
| スピッツ, R. A. | Spitz, René A. | 1887〜1974 | H |
| スピルバーガー, C. D. | Spielberger, Charles D. | 1927〜2013 | F |
| スペリー, R. W. | Sperry, Roger W. | 1913〜1994 | B J |
| セリエ, H. | Selye, Hans | 1907〜1982 | B |
| セリグマン, M. | Seligman, Martin | 1942〜 | B F I |
| ソーンダイク, E. L. | Thorndike, Edward L. | 1874〜1949 | C |

## た 行

| | | | |
|---|---|---|---|
| ダーウィン, C. | Darwin, Charles | 1809〜1882 | A H |
| タジフェル, H. | Tajfel, Henri | 1919〜1982 | I |
| ターマン, L. M. | Terman, Lewis M. | 1877〜1956 | G |
| タルヴィング, E. | Tulving, Endel | 1927〜 | D |
| タルビング, E. | ⇒タルヴィング, E. | | |
| チャルディーニ, R. B. | ⇒チャルディーン, R. B. | | |
| チャルディーン, R. B. | Cialdini, Robert B. | 1945〜 | I |
| チョムスキー, A. N. | Chomsky, Avram N. | 1928〜 | E |
| ディシ, E. L. | Deci, Edward L. | 1942〜 | C F I |
| ティチェナー, E. B. | ⇒ティッチナー, E. B. | | |
| ティチナー, E. B. | ⇒ティッチナー, E. B. | | |
| ティッチナー, E. B. | Titchener, Edward B. | 1867〜1927 | A |
| ティンバーゲン, N. | Tinbergen, Nikolaas | 1907〜1988 | C |
| ティンベルヘン, N. | ⇒ティンバーゲン, N. | | |
| デカルト, R. | Descartes, René | 1596〜1650 | A |
| デシ, E. L. | ⇒ディシ, E. L. | | |
| テッサー, A. | Tesser, Abraham | — | I J |
| デューイ, J. | Dewey, John | 1859〜1952 | A |
| テューキー, J. W. | Tukey, John W. | 1915〜2000 | K |
| デュマ, G. | Dumas, Georges | 1866〜1946 | A |
| ドイッチュ, M. | Deutsch, Morton | 1920〜2017 | J |
| ドーキンス, R. | Dawkins, Richard | 1941〜 | C |

| | | | |
|---|---|---|---|
| トールマン, E. C. | Tolman, Edward C. | 1886〜1957 | C |

## な 行

| | | | |
|---|---|---|---|
| ナイサー, U. | Neisser, Ulric | 1928〜2012 | B D |
| ニューカム, T. M. | Newcomb, Theodore M. | 1903〜1984 | I |

## は 行

| | | | |
|---|---|---|---|
| ハイダー, F. | Heider, Fritz | 1896〜1988 | I |
| バウアー, T. G. R. | Bower, Thomas G. R. | 1941〜2014 | B H |
| ハヴィガースト, R. J. | Havighurst, Robert J. | 1900〜1991 | H |
| ハーシ, T. | Hirschi, Travis | 1935〜2017 | J |
| パーソンズ, F. | Parsons, Frank | 1854〜1908 | H I J |
| パーソンズ, T. | Parsons, Talcott | 1902〜1979 | A I |
| バッドリー, A. D. | Baddeley, Alan D. | 1934〜 | D |
| バドリー, A. D. | ⇒バッドリー, A. D. | | |
| パブロフ, I. P. | Pavlov, Ivan P. | 1849〜1936 | A |
| ハミルトン, W. D. | Hamilton, William D. | 1936〜2000 | A C H I |
| ハル, C. L. | Hull, Clark L. | 1884〜1952 | C |
| ハーロウ, H. F. | Harlow, Harry F. | 1905〜1981 | C H |
| バーン, D. | Byrne, Donn | 1931〜2014 | G I |
| バーン, E. | Berne, Eric | 1910〜1970 | J |
| バンデューラ, A. | Bandura, Albert | 1925〜 | I |
| ピアジェ, J. | Piaget, Jean | 1896〜1980 | H |
| ピアソン, K. | Pearson, Karl | 1857〜1936 | K |
| ビネー, A. | Binet, Alfred | 1857〜1911 | G |
| ビューラー, C. | Bühler, Charlotte | 1893〜1974 | H |
| ビューラー, K. | Bühler, Karl | 1879〜1963 | H |
| ヒーリー, W. | Healy, William | 1869〜1963 | J |
| ヒルガード, E. R. | Hilgard, Ernest R. | 1904〜2001 | C F |
| ファンツ, R. L. | Fantz, Robert L. | 1925〜1981 | H |

フィッシャー

| | | | |
|---|---|---|---|
| フィッシャー, R. A. | Fisher, Ronald A. | 1890〜1962 | K |
| フェスティンガー, L. | Festinger, Leon | 1919〜1989 | I |
| フェスティンジャー, L. | ⇒フェスティンガー, L. | | |
| フェヒナー, G. T. | Fechner, Gustav T. | 1801〜1887 | A B |
| プラトン | Plato | B.C. 427〜 347 | A |
| フランクル, V. E. | Frankl, Viktor E. | 1905〜1997 | J |
| ブルーナー, J. S. | Bruner, Jerome S. | 1915〜2016 | B C D H |
| フレーベル, F. W. A. | Froebel, Friedrich W. A. | 1782〜1852 | H |
| プレマック, D. | Premack, David | 1925〜2015 | C H |
| フロイト, A. | Freud, Anna | 1895〜1982 | J |
| フロイト, S. | Freud, Sigmund | 1856〜1939 | J |
| ブローカ, P. P. | Broca, P. Paul | 1824〜1880 | B |
| ブロス, P. | Blos, Peter | 1904〜1997 | H J |
| ブロッカー, P. P. | ⇒ブローカ, P. P. | | |
| フロム, E. | Fromm, Erich | 1900〜1980 | I J |
| ブロンフェンブレンナー, U. | Bronfenbrenner, Urie | 1917〜2005 | H |
| ヘス, E. H. | Hess, Eckhard H. | 1916〜1986 | B F I |
| ベック, A. T. | Beck, Aaron T. | 1921〜 | J |
| ヘッブ, D. O. | Hebb, Donald O. | 1904〜1985 | B C |
| ベネディクト, R. F. | Benedict, Ruth F. | 1887〜1948 | I |
| ベム, D. J. | Bem, Daryl J. | 1938〜 | F G I |
| ベム, S. L. | Bem, Sandra L. | 1944〜2014 | G I |
| ヘルムホルツ, H. L. F. von | Helmholtz, Hermann L. F. von | 1821〜1894 | A B |
| ペンフィールド, W. G. | Penfield, Wilder G. | 1891〜1976 | B |
| ホイットニー, D. R. | Whitney, Donald R. | 1915〜2007 | K |
| ボウルビィ, J. | Bowlby, John | 1907〜1990 | H |
| ホーナイ, K. | Horney, Karen | 1885〜1952 | H J |
| ホブランド, C. I. | Hovland, Carl I. | 1912〜1961 | E I |
| ホランド, J. L. | Holland, John L. | 1919〜2008 | C I |

| ホール, G. S. | Hall, Granville S. | 1844〜1924 | A H |
| ボールドウィン, J. M. | Baldwin, James M. | 1861〜1934 | A H I |
| ポルトマン, A. | Portmann, Adolf | 1897〜1982 | H |

## ま 行

| マクドゥーガル, W. | McDougall, William | 1871〜1938 | F C |
| マクネマー, Q. | McNemar, Quinn | 1900〜1986 | K |
| マクレランド, D. C. | McClelland, David C. | 1917〜1998 | F |
| マクレランド, J. L. | McClelland, James L. | 1948〜 | D |
| マスロー, A. H. | ⇒マズロー, A. H. | | |
| マズロー, A. H. | Maslow, Abraham H. | 1908〜1970 | G |
| マックネマー, Q. | ⇒マクネマー, Q. | | |
| マッケイ, H. D. | McKay, Henry D. | 1899〜1980 | J |
| マートン, R. K. | Merton, Robert K. | 1910〜2003 | I J |
| マーラー, M. S. | Mahler, Margaret S. | 1897〜1985 | H J |
| マーレー, H. A. | Murray, Henry A. | 1893〜1988 | F J |
| マレー, H. A. | ⇒マーレー, H. A. | | |
| ミード, G. H. | Mead, George H. | 1863〜1931 | I |
| ミード, M. | Mead, Margaret | 1901〜1978 | I |
| ミューラー・リヤー, F. C. | Müller-Lyer, Franz C. | 1857〜1916 | B |
| ミュラー・リエル, F. C. | ⇒ミューラー・リヤー, F. C. | | |
| ミラー, G. A. | Miller, George A. | 1920〜2012 | D E |
| ミラー, N. E. | Miller, Neal E. | 1909〜2002 | C F |
| ミルグラム, S. | Milgram, Stanley | 1933〜1984 | I |
| メーラビアン, A. | Mehrabian, Albert | 1939〜 | F |
| メラビアン, A. | ⇒メーラビアン, A. | | |
| モレノ, J. L. | Moreno, Jacob L. | 1892〜1974 | J |
| モンテッソーリ, M. | Montessori, Maria | 1870〜1952 | H |

## や 行

| | | | |
|---|---|---|---|
| ヤスパース, K. | Jaspers, Karl | 1883～1969 | A |
| ユング, C. G. | Jung, Carl G. | 1875～1961 | J |

## ら 行

| | | | |
|---|---|---|---|
| ライプニッツ, G. W. von | Leibniz, Gottfried W. von | 1646～1716 | A |
| ラカン, J. | Lacan, Jacques | 1901～1981 | A |
| ラザルス, R. S. | Lazarus, Richard S. | 1922～2002 | B F J |
| ラタネ, B. | Latané, Bibb | 1937～ | I |
| ラメルハート, D. E. | Rumelhart, David E. | 1942～2011 | D |
| リカート, R. | Likert, Rensis | 1903～1981 | K |
| リッカート, R. | ⇒リカート, R. | | |
| ルソー, J. | Rousseau, Jean-Jacques | 1712～1778 | A H |
| ルビン, E. J. | Rubin, Edgar J. | 1886～1951 | A B |
| ルーメルハート, D. E. | ⇒ラメルハート, D. E. | | |
| ルメルハート, D. E. | ⇒ラメルハート, D. E. | | |
| ルリア, A. R. | Luria, Alexander R. | 1902～1977 | E |
| レヴィン, K. | Lewin, Kurt | 1890～1947 | I |
| レヴィンソン, D. J. | Levinson, Daniel J. | 1920～1994 | G |
| ロジャーズ, C. R. | Rogers, Carl R. | 1902～1987 | J |
| ローゼンサール, R. | Rosenthal, Robert | 1933～ | I |
| ローゼンソール, R. | ⇒ローゼンサール, R. | | |
| ローゼンタール, R. | ⇒ローゼンサール, R. | | |
| ローゼンツワイク, S. | Rosenzweig, Saul | 1907～2004 | F G I |
| ローゼンバーグ, M. J. | Rosenberg, Morris J. | 1922～1992 | G I |
| ロック, J. | Locke, John | 1632～1704 | A H |
| ロッター, J. B. | Rotter, Julian B. | 1916～2014 | C |
| ロフタス, E. F. | Loftus, Elizabeth F. | 1944～ | D I J |
| ロールシャッハ, H. | Rorschach, Hermann | 1884～1922 | J |
| ローレンツ, K. | Lorenz, Konrad | 1903～1989 | C |

| ロンブローゾ, C. | Lombroso, Cesare | 1836～1909 | J |

## わ 行

| ワイナー, B. | Weiner, Bernard | 1935～ | I |
| ワトソン, J. B. | Watson, John B. | 1878～1958 | C |
| ワロン, H. P. H. | Wallon, Henri P. H. | 1879～1962 | H |

## 著者 (五十音順)・専門分野

| | |
|---|---|
| 安藤　明人（あんどう　あきひと） | 社会心理学＊ |
| 井上　雅勝（いのうえ　まさかつ） | 認知心理学 |
| 小花和 Wright 尚子（おばなわ ライト なおこ） | 発達心理学＊ |
| 齊藤　文夫（さいとう　ふみお） | 犯罪心理学 |
| 佐方　哲彦（さかた　てつひこ） | 青年臨床心理学＊ |
| 杉村　省吾（すぎむら　しょうご） | 臨床心理学 |
| 松村　憲一（まつむら　けんいち） | 情報社会心理学 |

（＊＝編者）

　この用語集は，まだ完璧なものではありません。より使いやすく，わかりやすいものにしていくことを目指しています。修正すべき点や不適切な点がありましたら，ご連絡いただければ幸いです。

---

**連絡先**　〒663-8558　兵庫県西宮市池開町6-46
　　　　　武庫川女子大学文学部心理・社会福祉学科
　　　　　学科準備室　TEL　0798-45-9811
　　　　　学科サイト　http://www.mukogawa-u.ac.jp/~ningen/

**心理学英和・和英基本用語集**

2010 年 3 月 30 日　初版第 1 刷発行
2019 年 12 月 1 日　　第 5 刷発行

| | |
|---|---|
| 編著者 | 小花和 Wright 尚子 |
| | 安藤　明人 |
| | 佐方　哲彦 |
| 発行者 | 宮下　基幸 |
| 発行所 | 福村出版株式会社 |

〒113-0034　東京都文京区湯島2-14-11
電話　03-5812-9702　FAX 03-5812-9705
https://www.fukumura.co.jp

印刷　モリモト印刷株式会社
製本　協栄製本株式会社

©N. Obanawa W., A. Ando, T. Sakata 2010
Printed in Japan
ISBN978-4-571-20075-5 C3011
定価はカバーに表示してあります。

# 現代社会と応用心理学〈全7巻〉

日本応用心理学会 企画／藤田主一・浮谷秀一 編
現代社会と応用心理学 1

## クローズアップ「学校」

◎2,400円　ISBN978-4-571-25501-4　C3311

目まぐるしく変化する現代社会に対応を迫られる学校。現場で何が起きているのか，「こころ」の問題を探る。

---

日本応用心理学会 企画／大坊郁夫・谷口泰富 編
現代社会と応用心理学 2

## クローズアップ「恋愛」

◎2,400円　ISBN978-4-571-25502-1　C3311

若者の恋愛，同性愛，おとなの恋愛，結婚，離婚，浮気，夫婦関係，家族……現代社会の恋愛にフォーカス！

---

日本応用心理学会 企画／玉井 寛・内藤哲雄 編
現代社会と応用心理学 3

## クローズアップ「健康」

◎2,400円　ISBN978-4-571-25503-8　C3311

現代日本社会における健康に関わるトピックを，現実的で多面的な視点から捉え，応用心理学的な解説を試みる。

---

日本応用心理学会 企画／森下高治・蓮花一己・向井希宏 編
現代社会と応用心理学 4

## クローズアップ「メンタルヘルス・安全」

◎2,400円　ISBN978-4-571-25504-5　C3311

現代社会における職場や日常生活でのメンタルヘルス，ヒューマンエラー，リスクマネジメントを考える。

---

日本応用心理学会 企画／浮谷秀一・大坊郁夫 編
現代社会と応用心理学 5

## クローズアップ「メディア」

◎2,400円　ISBN978-4-571-25505-2　C3311

日々目まぐるしく変化を遂げるメディア。21世紀の現代社会と人間関係を象徴するトピックが満載。

---

日本応用心理学会 企画／内藤哲雄・玉井 寛 編
現代社会と応用心理学 6

## クローズアップ「高齢社会」

◎2,400円　ISBN978-4-571-25506-9　C3311

現代日本社会の象徴といえる高齢社会の現実的様相を多面的な視点から捉え，応用心理学的な解説を展開する。

---

日本応用心理学会 企画／谷口泰富・藤田主一・桐生正幸 編
現代社会と応用心理学 7

## クローズアップ「犯罪」

◎2,400円　ISBN978-4-571-25507-6　C3311

犯罪心理はもとより，現代の犯罪の特徴から犯罪をとりまく事象を25のトピックで解説。現代社会の本質に迫る。

◎価格は本体価格です。